Money Problems and Pastoral Care

Paul G. Schurman

Fortress Press   **Philadelphia**

Creative Pastoral Care and Counseling Series
  Editor: Howard J. Clinebell
  Associate Editor: Howard W. Stone

To Ralph and Edith Schurman

COPYRIGHT © 1982 BY FORTRESS PRESS

Library of Congress Cataloging in Publication Data

Schurman, Paul G.
  Money problems and pastoral care.

  (Creative pastoral care and counseling series)
  Bibliography: p.
  1. Pastoral counseling. 2. Finance, Personal.
3. Clergy—Finance, Personal. I. Title. II. Series.
BV4012.2.S37   332.024′2   81–70662
ISBN 0–8006–0568–3   AACR2

9414A82   Printed in the United States of America   1–568

Contents

Series Foreword

Let me share with you some of the hopes that are in the minds of those of us who helped to develop this series—hopes that relate directly to you as the reader. It is our desire and expectation that these books will be of help to you in developing better working tools as a minister-counselor. We hope that they will do this by encouraging your own creativity in developing new methods and counsel for helping people live life more fully. It is our intention in this series to affirm the many things you have going for you as a minister in helping troubled persons—the many assets and resources from your religious heritage, your role as the leader of a congregation, and your unique relationship to individuals and families throughout the life cycle. We hope to help you reaffirm the *power of the pastoral* by the use of fresh models and methods in your ministry.

The aim of the series is not to be comprehensive with respect to topics but rather to bring innovative approaches to some major types of counseling. Although the books are practice-oriented, they also provide a solid foundation of theological and psychological insights. They are written primarily for ministers (and those preparing for the ministry) but we hope that they will also prove useful to other counselors who are interested in the crucial role of spiritual and value issues in all helping relationships. In addition we hope that the series will be useful in seminary courses, clergy support groups, continuing education workshops, and lay befriender training.

This is a period of rich new developments in counseling and psychotherapy. The time is ripe for a flowering of creative methods and insights in pastoral care and counseling. Our expectation is that this series will stimulate grass-roots creativity as innovative methods and programs come alive for you. Some of the major thrusts that will be discussed in this series include a new awareness of the unique contribution of the theologically trained counselor, the liberating power of the human potentials orientation, an appreciation of the pastoral care function of the ministering congregation, the importance of humanizing systems and institutions as well as close relationships, the importance of pastoral *care* (and not just counseling), the many opportunities for caring ministries throughout the life cycle, the deep changes in male-female relationships occurring today, and the new psychotherapies such as Gestalt therapy, Transactional Analysis, educative counseling, and crisis methods. Our hope is that this series will enhance your resources for your ministry to persons by opening doorways to understanding of these creative thrusts in pastoral care and counseling.

In this book Paul Schurman throws light on a crucial, oft-neglected area of pastoral counseling and education—financial problems. The author has expertise in family systems theory and in the practice of marriage and family counseling. He believes that religious institutions have a clear responsibility to help both single individuals and families learn how to cope constructively with our economically perilous times of chronic inflation and shrinking resources. This book provides the principles and practical methods for fulfilling this responsibility.

A basic strength of the book is its dual objective. The author holds that only as we clergy practice sound financial management ourselves will we gain the credibility and expertise needed to counsel and educate others in this important area of living. Therefore, the book provides insights and guidelines to help busy pastors with their own financial problems and planning. In addition it aims at helping pastors not only in their counseling with individuals and families facing financial crises, but also in providing effective educational programs designed to help people *prevent* such crises by learning how to handle the stressful and perplexing fiscal realities of our contemporary world.

As a theologically trained counselor and educator, the author offers biblical guidelines for sound financial planning and decision making. At the same time, he sees the complex interrelationship of family dynamics and values with family financial behavior. In light of this awareness, he highlights sound principles for creating a workable financial plan, stressing the importance of whole-family participation in the planning process. Paul has a keen interest in intentional life-styling, in the growth of families through the life cycle. This longitudinal orientation becomes a valuable perspective as he traces the changing fiscal needs of a family through the stages of their journey together. He also recognizes and discusses the special financial problems faced by women and singles in our male-controlled, marriage-oriented society.

In exploring the complex relationship between marital conflict and money, a helpful distinction is made between financial counseling per se and counseling where family economic problems are symptomatic of deeper relationship problems. Pastoral counseling on financial issues, as the author describes it, is grounded in an awareness of family dynamics and of fiscal reality. It is also grounded in an understanding of the ways in which money management reflects an individual's or family's guiding values. Thus, pastoral education and counseling in this area seeks to help persons clarify and revise their values to reflect constructive religious norms in our global society.

The author suggests practical approaches to a variety of financial issues with which most people struggle—taxes, the use of credit, life insurance, consumer issues, helping children learn fiscal responsibilities, retirement. He also focuses on the special financial issues faced by clergy families, including negotiating with a congregation for appropriate remuneration, special clergy tax considerations, and planning for housing after retirement. The last section of the book aims at helping a busy pastor develop a solid educational program of financial planning through the life cycle, using resource people available in community and church. Several working models of educational events are described, with guidelines for designing and evaluating such events.

Paul Schurman has taught pastoral counseling at the School of Theology at Claremont, California, since 1974. He is also a clinical director of the Pomona Valley Pastoral Counseling and Growth Centers. Before coming to Claremont he counseled with clergy families and did continuing education in pastoral care and counseling for six years for the East Ohio Conference of the United Methodist Church. His experience there provided much of his in-depth understanding of clergy-related financial problems and their solutions. Before serving in Ohio, Paul pastored churches in the San Francisco area. During the years of our colleagueship at the School of Theology, I have come to esteem Paul's professional competence and prize our friendship.

I predict that this book will be a valuable resource for a variety of groups. Pastors will find it useful both in their counseling and in their personal financial planning. They will surely want to use it in marriage preparation sessions with couples. Educational leaders interested in strengthening family life will find the book helpful in relation to classes and workshops aimed at assisting persons in implementing Christian stewardship in their life-styles. Lay persons involved in occupations such as banking and accounting may use it to help their clients understand the interpersonal and value contexts of fiscal problems. Specialists in pastoral counseling, and those charged with being pastor to pastors, can use the book's suggestions to help some clergy replace the financial chaos in their lives with a measure of reasonable order.

My encounter with Paul's manuscript has made me more aware of the many ways in which caring, including pastoral caring, can be embodied in the mundane issues surrounding money. Personally I found the book a constructive confrontation with my own need to do more planning (hopefully, astute) in an area where I have tended to "fly by the seat of my pants." My hope and expectation is that you will find this book helpful both professionally and personally in the earthy arena of finances—an arena in which spiritual issues abound, often in disguise.

HOWARD CLINEBELL

Preface

Tom Brown is a forty-year-old pastor of a suburban church. Tom and Marcia live with their two grade-school-age children in a nice parsonage in an affluent community close to a large city. Most of the people earn at least half again as much as Tom. He and Marcia often feel the pressure to "keep up" with their more affluent neighbors. Much of the pressure comes from their children, who simply do not understand why they can live in such a nice house yet not afford all the things that their schoolmates enjoy. The Browns feel out of place with the success-oriented life-style of their neighbors.

They have discussed moving to an urban parish, but are concerned about the children's education and safety. Tom and Marcia enjoy his secure base salary plus some attractive fringe benefits. But they have not been able to save much for the children's college. The Browns dream of owning their own home, but that possibility looks increasingly remote in today's housing market.

Their most tense moments occur during discussions about the family budget. Marcia worries aloud that they do not save more, recalling her parents' admonition to "save for a rainy day." Tom feels he is being criticized for not earning more; he remembers his parents saying, "You can't take it with you."

Recently, Marcia has taken a part-time job three days a week, working from 3:00 to 11:00 P.M. Tom now cares for the children while Marcia is at work. He frets about not spending enough time on church work and is indignant at having to take over some of the household duties.

Marcia would like to complete her college degree but is not sure they can afford it. She resents not having this opportunity. In a recent discussion about finances, she exclaimed, "Tom, I just don't think we know where we are going." And Tom added wistfully, "Or how we are going to get there either."

This is not an uncommon story. As a pastoral counselor of clergy for six years, I have listened to many variations on this theme. Not many clergy were ever taught financial planning, and after all, was not the ministry a vocational choice that tended to allow one to avoid concern with the material world of dollars and property?

Money management is a growing problem for individuals and families across the country. Some marriage counselors estimate that half the families who come to them for help have money problems, and that nearly 9 out of 10 persons who divorce suffer conflict with money. Ray Fowler, executive director of the American Association of Marriage and Family Therapists, claims that the biggest problem facing families today is that of finances; in spite of our having considerably more education than our parents had, it now takes two salaries to survive, whereas a generation ago families could maintain a middle-class standard on one income.

For more than a decade economic, social, political, technological, and environmental changes have seriously impacted the social and economic well-being of our people. Though there have been improvements in the quality of life for some, others have found that even a doubled income has failed to increase their purchasing power. Many have been forced to a lower standard of living. This is especially true if the income is provided by a female head of household. In such families the buying power of the income has slipped about 50 percent in ten years. Retired persons with fixed incomes have been hit harder than those whose incomes were more flexible. Minority incomes also have lagged considerably behind their white counterparts.

According to the polls, vast segments of society think family life has gotten worse in the last fifteen years, and most cite the cost of living as the biggest problem facing families today. The loss of buying power causes us to feel that our options are limited. It breeds a sense of powerlessness. Times of economic stress result in more child abuse and battered parents. According to a recent study, more than half the people over sixty say they are living a "hand-to-mouth" existence because of financial pressures.*

We used to approach economic problems with more of everything—more work hours, higher wages, increased consumption—but today's world requires an emphasis on educating ourselves and others for more efficient and responsible use of all our resources.

This book attempts to help religious leaders integrate sound biblical guidelines for the management of resources with some contemporary tools and designs in financial planning.

Why a book on financial planning for religious leaders? There are several reasons. Religious leaders will benefit both personally and professionally from training in financial planning. It is obvious that if religious leaders are to be helpful to individuals and families in this area, they need to give some attention to getting their own house in order. Results of a study done while I was serving as a counselor to clergy revealed that very few clergy do much financial planning. For example, nearly 75 percent of the clergy families involved in this study had made no plans for housing their families in the event of unexpected death or retirement.*

There are additional reasons for directing a book on financial planning to religious leaders: ministers possess a concern for strengthening family life; they work in the context of a values framework which is crucial for financial planning; many persons readily turn to religious leaders for care or counseling at times of crisis; the religious community engages individuals and families in educational endeavors at all age levels and is involved with persons at the change-points in their lives—birth, baptism, marriage, and death, all of which include potential financial crises; and the religious community contains most of the essential ingredients for good financial planning, including a variety of resource persons.

This book is not intended to make financial experts out of religious leaders. Rather, it aims to (1) be of direct help to these leaders and their families in the area of financial planning; (2) help sharpen diagnostic skills that can stimulate awareness of the interpersonal implications of financial planning; (3) increase awareness of the relationship between financial planning and family stability; (4) enhance counseling expertise with respect to financial crises; (5) refine sensitivity to the important life-cycle change-points as opportunities for ministry with respect to the issues of money and values, and (6) define and explain the steps in designing effective financial-planning educational programs based on religious values. Only as clergy practice sound financial planning themselves will they gain the expertise and authenticity to counsel and educate others in this area.

1. Money in the Family

This is a book about money and families. Because the definition of family is in great flux today, some clarification is necessary at the outset.

The Changing Family

Futurist author Alvin Toffler in his latest book, *The Third Wave,* depicts the current dazzling diversity of ways to live together.* The family is not dying. It is simply taking on a plurality of forms, not only in western societies but to some extent also even in Eastern Europe and other parts of the world.

In 1950, over 80 percent of American households were made up of two or more persons related by blood, marriage, or adoption, and the vast majority of these households resembled closely the image of the traditional nuclear family with a mother and father and two children. Since the 1950s, however, the proportion of households consisting of unrelated individuals or single persons has more than doubled, and today about one of every four households is composed of persons who are living either alone or with non-relatives.†

The nuclear family still survives. It still serves many people well. But it is no longer the norm against which all other family forms must be measured. Alongside the traditional family, there is now a variety of new household structures.

Marie Wilson, age sixty-seven, lives alone in a small apartment in a Midwestern city. Marie's husband, Alex, who retired from the ministry several years ago, recently died. Upon Alex's death, Marie sold their home and moved into an apartment building where several other retired persons resided. She volunteers several hours a week, serving lunch to senior citizens at a nearby church, and since she is the only one with a car, she drives her circle of friends to church, to the market, and wherever else they decide to go.

Bob Friend, age thirty-three, came west a few years ago for graduate studies with his wife, Fran, and son, Bobby. Two years ago Bob and Fran separated. Bobby, in the joint custody of both parents, now lives part-time with each one.

Within several blocks of where I live, there is a household consisting of Judy, Mark, Samantha, Jill, and Peter. Graduate students at the university, these single young adults share a home, hold part-time jobs in the community, and consider their living arrangement as an economic alternative to dormitory rooms or small apartments. They all contribute to the rent, food, and utilities, and they all share in the common responsibility of running the home.

Add to these examples the child-free couples, single-parent households, trial marriages, two-career couples, and homosexual couples, and you begin to get a sense of the growing diversity in family structures. It is becoming ever clearer that the family of the future will consist of smaller, more flexible units than were common a generation ago.

Even the high rate of divorce today does not signal the demise of the family but only adds another feature to its complexity. Very few persons stay divorced. Increasingly, divorced persons remarry, bringing children from previous marriages into their new families.

There are some indications that the trend toward divorce may be reversing to some extent. More and more people are recognizing that though a marriage may be bad, divorce can be even worse. Divorce is no longer considered the automatic solution for a troubled marriage. An increasing number of persons are choosing less radical treatment, such as marriage counseling. Money may be one major reason for this: it is no longer possible for the average family to maintain two households.

In addition to the economic deterrent to divorce there is a growing recognition of the pain and trauma that attend it. People are beginning to think twice before opting to terminate their marriage. Research suggests that though divorce need not always result in psychological trauma, it does carry with it considerable risk of such a reaction, for adults as well as for children. Judith Wallerstein and Joan Kelley found that even five years after divorce 31 percent of the fathers and 42 percent of the mothers had not achieved psychological or social stability and that 37 percent of the children were moderately depressed.* This risk of trauma accompanying divorce is becoming better known to the general public.

No, for all its problems—and dazzling diversity—the family is still very much alive and functioning. But it is changing. And in our discussion of family economics, we shall need to keep in focus this pluralism in family configuration.

Economics and Family Stability

There is a close tie between economics and family stability. The state of the economy and the well-being of the home go hand in hand. "Recession," "inflation," "unemployment" are chilling words to most of us. Waiting in gas lines, opening utility bills, helping children with college costs, shopping at the supermarket to feed a family—such experiences give these frightening words added immediacy. To those who have either lost a job or face the prospect of that terrible reality, the situation is grim indeed!

When the costs of basic necessities—such as food, shelter, clothing, and medical care—escalate, absorbing an ever greater proportion of income, the emotional and even physical distress of our financial concerns is compounded. These harsh economic realities increase the vulnerability of many single individuals and families, especially those whose earnings are marginal. Beyond the actual economic losses attributable to inflation, there are also psychological losses. Author Robert Fuller points out that "even in a system that provided complete and perfect protection against all the economic consequences, people would still object to inflation, if for no other reason than that stable, reliable prices offer a kind of security. The passing of the ten-cent cup of coffee feels like the death of an old friend."†

I talked at length recently with a number of clergy couples from my local area and tried to assess their feelings about family life today, especially with respect to the effects of inflation on family stability. Representing a variety of faith groups, ethnic groups, ages, and marital and vocational statuses, these couples were generally hopeful about the future of the family, although aware that it is in much ferment today. They made a number of observations based on their own personal experience:

Families are floundering, many of them caught up in agonizing role adjustments and societal value shifts, not at all clear about the nature of the ideal family. Some parents, with grown children living together outside of marriage, struggle to keep the lines of communication open between the generations. Women, much freer today, are no longer so exclusively the hub of family life. Children have less supervision, particularly in one-parent families or where both parents are working. Leaving home early is more common, particularly among low-income families but increasingly also among middle-income families. Some families are now pushing children out of the nest early as a result of inflation—and for the same reason these young people are having a harder time succeeding on their own. Runaway inflation has young people asking, "What have I done wrong?"* Despite college degrees and hard work, they are still unable to enter the economic mainstream as measured by the traditional prerequisites of home and automobile ownership.

The clergy couples I talked with confirmed the close tie between economics and family stability: families need help with their values; they need models for family growth. To raise a family that will embrace your own values is ever more of a challenge. It requires struggle to counteract the predominant cultural values relating to money and possessions, and the power of the mass media to impact the family's values. On television "you see so much you never knew you needed," commented one parent. "We lack imaginative images of family," said another. "We have more, we want more, until we are way over our heads," added yet another parent.

The rate of inflation in recent years has compounded the problem for families. One mother said, "I find myself getting angry at the children just for growing, since growing means new clothes, and clothes are so expensive." In many instances, both spouses have to work to make ends meet, and even then, as one put it: "Outgo always equals income." An economically troubled family is generally in much greater peril of disintegration. As far as family life is concerned, inflation means stress. "Inflation this year has been a killer," exclaimed one parent.

Where both parents are working, time for family concerns becomes more limited. In some instances time may be even a greater problem than money. "The trend," one parent commented, "is to work more to get more, and the result is less time for the family."

Clergy families who talked with me were careful not to complain or sound too bitter about their own economic picture. Although clergy remuneration has improved over the years, it is still inadequate and considerably below the level of other professions, particularly for minority pastors. Most clergy favor home ownership as a hedge against inflation and as a necessary preparation for retirement. The housing situation and family size are critical determinants when it comes to managing on a minister's salary. Increasingly clergy spouses are employed full-time. The clergy couples I spoke with do little financial planning. Those who do, while they may have some long-range goals, or at least hopes, nonetheless tend to operate on the basis of only weekly or monthly planning.

Money and Planning

Our culture tends to place great value on money. To one person, money is power; to another, status; and to yet another, mobility or pleasure. Nearly all of us see money as a means of security—if only we can accumulate enough of it! But there is the rub: how much is enough? The usual answer to that question is "just a little bit more," no matter what the level of income may be. Money alone, however, does not guarantee happiness.* The way it is used is far more determinative; it can serve as a stabilizing factor in a family, or it can prove to be the focal point for conflict. One thing is sure: money is a very important commodity in most modern families.

Its importance in daily living has been enhanced with the move away from the country to the city, as the distance between production and consumption has increased. Today we do not "make" a living—we earn it. Goods change hands more frequently and the medium of exchange is money. We have to apportion our income so as to acquire the goods someone else produces.

The increased use of money suggests that it not be employed haphazardly. Unfortunately, many people view financial planning as a restriction of their freedom. Actually, such planning functions much as a dam that holds back the unrestricted flow of a river so as to direct its water into channels that can supply power as the need arises. Rather than being restrictive, then, a plan can function as a means toward achieving one's goals.

Informal financial planning goes on to some extent in almost every family. However, there may be resistance to an involvement of the entire household in such planning. In part, this is simply because old habits are hard to break. In part, too, it is because any shift in an accepted family practice results in a shift of power. There is a certain amount of threat connected with any change, particularly when that change is one over which we have little or no control. However, in spite of the risk of temporarily increasing family anxiety, financial planning that involves the entire family in the process will strengthen that family and help it adjust to the multitude of external changes bombarding it from every direction.

The way you as a pastor feel about money is extremely important. To the extent that the pastor's own money affairs are haphazard, or his or her attitudes about it confused, the process of helping others will be seriously impeded. It is imperative, therefore, to begin with your own family and initiate some dialogue: What are the goals and purposes of this family? What do you want to happen for the family collectively and for each of its members? What resources do you possess, and how can you better utilize them toward the realization of your objectives?

Involving the entire family in such deliberation means that ultimately, in matters of money, no family member is seen as an employee who must have a requisition slip signed by a superior. Rather, each family member assumes the role of a stockholder, with voting power reflective of age and experience. Participation and responsibility in planning is the best way to avoid careless use of money and help the family navigate through difficult days. Such sharing provides an excellent training program for youngsters who may well be facing even more difficult economic problems in the years ahead.

Clarifying Values

It is at the point of transferring the family's values to the children that family financial planning takes on tremendous importance. Far too many parents assume that training in positive values occurs automatically in the very process of raising the children—or perhaps takes place at church. Values are indeed transmitted in these settings, but sometimes we unwittingly teach conflicting values.

The important thing is to be more intentional and explicit with our children about what we value and desire to teach.

At one time or another most of us have probably said: "I'd sure do some things differently if I had the chance to raise my kids again." Chuck and Barbara actually have that opportunity. They are in a second marriage. Chuck, age fifty-two, has been in the ministry for twenty-seven years, while Barbara, age thirty-five, has recently completed seminary. Chuck took a significant salary cut to relocate in support of Barbara's education, and the couple will soon take a further cut in order to share a copastorate where each will be involved half-time.

The first marriages of both were considerably more traditional. It is clear to Chuck that he was ambitiously pursuing the "American Dream" (which is mirrored in the goals and expectations of middle-class males in other western societies). His hard work was rewarded with promotions, but problems developed because each promotion demanded more time away from his family. Paradoxically, the harder Chuck worked to provide more and better for his family, the more alienated he became from his roles as husband and father, and the more his family life suffered.

Their first marriages taught Chuck and Barbara many things about the relationship between economics and family stability. Even as money does not guarantee happiness, so money alone does not guarantee stability. The way money is used and the underlying family values expressed in that usage are more crucial. Chuck and Barbara are aware, too, that earning less money will not ensure happiness either. However, the time made available by sharing a job will give them the opportunity to be more involved with Barbara's two children from her previous marriage.

Chuck is determined to do things differently this time. For one thing, the financial planning and decisions are now shared. Since there is less money, this family must be more creative in finding less expensive ways to support high-quality family life. Barbara feels that "buying into the American Dream and trying to do it on a clergy salary can be a trap." This couple does not have all the answers, but they know what is at stake; and they are using careful forethought in their planning.

Philip Zimbardo of Stanford University writes about our times that the Devil's strategy is "to trivialize human existence and to isolate us from one another while creating the delusion that the reasons are time pressures, work demands, or economic anxieties."* Zimbardo thinks that an economic downturn can be a blessing in disguise. He explains that since parents cannot easily afford divorce, they may discover some common values. This is more likely if they seek professional counseling, which many today are discovering can be not only far less expensive than divorce but also far less painful. Since more children are likely to return home for awhile after college, families must become more flexible in structure. With less money available, sharing may replace some of the hoarding; caring may supplant some of the flaunting. Zimbardo recommends that meantime we might reevaluate the survival strategies that many of the poor—immigrants, blacks, and other minorities—have used when money was soft and times were hard. While recognizing their vulnerability to the system and its power to overwhelm them, these groups have maintained much of their dignity by reaffirming family values and by tightening the bonds of friendship.

A good place for the family to begin its togetherness in planning is with an exploration of its values. The New Testament concept of stewardship provides a sound basis for such a values discussion.

Stewardship in the New Testament

There is a close connection between family financial planning and Christian stewardship. The connection is found in the idea of *oikonomia,* the Greek root of our English word "economics." However, while economics has become a science that studies the many factors affecting production, distribution, and the use of the world's resources, *oikonomia* referred simply to the ordinary management decisions made in every household. The New Testament steward functioned like one of the family. Unlike a servant or slave who simply followed directions, the steward was expected to exercise intelligence and initiative.

Jesus communicates this idea in the parable of the faithful and unfaithful stewards (Luke 12:42–48). The faithful steward is the sensibly prudent one, whom the master will set over the household. Such faithfulness will be rewarded with greater responsibilities, while the unfaithful and negligent steward will be punished. According to Jesus' parables, stewards were held accountable for the use they made of the resources entrusted to their care. Jesus was clearly looking for stewards who would be faithful and prudent in household management and the management of all resources.

Only persons and families who believe that the earth is the Lord's are able to experience the joyful gratitude and generosity of Christian stewardship. We can be faithful managers of our affairs because God is a faithful manager of creation: "We love, because God first loves us" (1 John 4:19).

Christian stewardship is not easy to practice. Contemporary values as reflected in the mass media are a constant source of seduction to covetousness, the idolatrous worship of money and material possessions. Jesus warned: "Take heed, and beware of all covetousness; for a man's life does not consist in the abundance of his possessions" (Luke 12:15). Try telling that to the credit manager at your bank. Our world insists on the importance of one's possessions. So we are in conflict over the discrepancy in values.

Jesus taught: "You cannot serve God and mammon" (Luke 16:13). The Aramaic word for "mammon" (well known by Jesus and his listeners because Aramaic was their native tongue) referred to wealth, property, money, and profit. Even though mammon was not to be served, Jesus never spoke disparagingly of it. He took it seriously because he knew that mammon had important instrumental value. Bread and houses and sandals and robes were important to Jesus. He knew that possessions could be used for God's purposes.

It is dangerous for a person to lean too heavily on money and possessions and identify his or her own worth with the value of these possessions. In this sense, money is no different from beauty or power or status or talent or race or sex or nationality or any other attribute that the world may value and in which one may attempt to gain a feeling of security. Someone has said that you can possess only what you are not afraid to lose. This is as true of relationships as it is of possessions. Indeed, whenever you treat a relationship as a possession, you put it in grave jeopardy. Anything that possesses you, you are not free to enjoy. To enjoy and appreciate a thing or a person, you must view your relationship to it as that of a steward, not an owner. This is why accumulation of possessions can so readily become oppressive.

Jesus spoke about management decisions in his parables. He pointed to people who practiced poor management, such as the rich farmer who built bigger barns while his life was coming to an end (Luke 12:16–21), the foolish maidens who ran out of oil before the bridegroom arrived (Matt. 25:1–13), and the man who built a house on the sand, where it was not able to withstand the storms (Matt. 7:26–27). Jesus' condemnation was based on the negligence or imprudence of their stewardship. The solutions they had opted for were not creative. The good steward is one who practices sensible and skillful administration in all affairs, keeping priorities clear.

Jesus had high praise for Mary of Bethany when she poured a jar of expensive ointment on his feet. The disciples were sharply critical of her extravagant act of love. "Why was this ointment not sold for three hundred denarii and given to the poor?" Judas asked (John 12:5). It was a legitimate question, since 300 denarii represented a year's income for an average laborer. However, Jesus did not measure prudence by business judgment alone. He knew that other values—such as the praise of God's Messiah—must sometimes take precedence. "She has done a beautiful thing," was his simple response (Mark 14:6). The lesson Jesus taught was one of prudent management exercised with a view to appropriate giving. Giving away what you have makes you part of all you share, and the joy of the gift is the reward you keep forever. Giving frees us to receive what others give. Reaching out to another moves us close enough to be touched.

Wants and Needs

One outgrowth of values clarification is the sharpening of the distinction between wants and needs. Knowing what you can get along without is as important as knowing what you must have. It has been said that a person is rich in proportion to the number of things he or she can afford to leave alone.

There is a simple values-clarification exercise you can use yourself or with your family.* It offers a good way to facilitate the dialogue and zero in on the important questions related to wanting and needing. From the list of eighteen values below, let each member of your family select the five values he or she prizes most highly:

A Comfortable Life	Inner Harmony
An Exciting Life	Mature Love
A Sense of Accomplishment	National Security
A World of Peace	Pleasure
A World of Beauty	Salvation
Equality	Self-respect
Family Security	Social Recognition
Freedom	True Friendship
Happiness	Wisdom

Have each person rank the selected items from one through five in order of perceived importance, and then place a dollar sign by those that either require money or influence its use. Now you are ready for a family discussion, beginning with a general sharing by each family member. Depending on the age level of your children, you can modify the list above to include relevant categories and terms each one will understand. Be sure to pursue the distinction between wants and needs.

Values-clarification exercises are also excellent for use in the educational enterprises of your church.* Chapter 6 will elaborate further on the use of such experiential learning in seminars and workshops.

Creative Decision Making

Once your values are clearly defined, you are in a position to exercise some creativity in decision making. There may be ways in which you can actually cut down on certain items in your regular spending pattern while at the same time achieving a value gain: eating less, for example, and thereby achieving a desired weight loss and an increase in health status; riding a bicycle or walking to work some of the time to save fuel expense, and thereby improving your physical condition; substituting a home family activity for the usual dinner out or movie, thus saving money and increasing family interaction.

In place of an hour of our usual TV watching, my wife, Anne, and I have begun taking some long evening walks after the southern California smog blows away and the temperature goes down.

This new activity saves a little electrical energy and provides us with some needed exercise. It is also a tension reducer, giving us an hour away from the children to talk and catch up on our days— not a bad exchange.

Family Values in Context

Family values do not exist in a vacuum. Every family is part of a complex ecosystem, in which it both affects and is affected by the environment. Nations are beginning to recognize their interdependence with other nations, large and small, and with the human-made and natural environments as well. These interfaces no longer involve merely abstract social or political issues. They affect the family directly. And the place to begin to effect change in the big picture is right here in your own family.

You may think you are powerless to change things, but consider that even industrial giants have been brought to their knees before the changed buying patterns of the general public. Even politicians are dependent for crucial policy actions on broad public support. You do have power! You are a far more important cog in the decision-making process than you may realize.

Families are becoming more sophisticated about the issues of the natural environment: the finiteness of resources such as fossil fuels; the pollution of water, land, and air; land use policy with respect to agricultural production and reforestation; food production policy, both nationally and in global assistance programs, and energy production methods—nuclear, coal, gasohol, solar. These same families are learning a good bit about the human-made environment and the ways it is influenced through the rules and decisions made in the judicial, educational, political, economic, religious, and family subsystems.

In addition, there is the human environment, where attitudes and values concerning money, work, responsibility, leisure, and life-style are created. This is the arena where goals are set, knowledge and skills are taught, and experience is gained and disseminated through our educational institutions, the family, and the media. Families are not islands. They are linked to each other. How each person and each family manages human and natural resources determines the quality of life and impacts the community, the nation, and the world.

Most persons have not stopped to ponder the relationship between the single detached housing unit and the utilization of resources, or the total costs of divorce in terms of maintaining two households, or the economic costs of certain housing arrangements for the elderly. These issues affect not only society as a whole but individual families as well—which is another reason why families should be involved in the social-action ministry at their church.

Economic decisions do not always involve separating the right from the wrong and the good from the bad. Economists explain that choices often involve looking at the benefits and costs of any two things, deciding which is the better of the two, and choosing accordingly. This economic principle is theologically viable as long as "cost and benefits" are examined in a broad enough manner. Some persons think of the cost-effectiveness principle only in terms of dollars and cents, choosing whatever option is more profitable. That perspective is too narrow. In fact, the problem often lies precisely in our human tendency to decide exclusively on the basis of political or economic expediency. The social scandals of the recent past, from employee thefts and corporation bribes to political tricks and payoffs, document the fact that it is our public ethic that has gone awry. As individuals, we are probably no more or less moral today than we ever were. The trouble lies rather in the malfunctioning of our secular public ethic.

The Protestant Ethic and the American Dream

The increased affluence since World War Two has contributed to the problem. The production or work or thrift ethic functioned reasonably well until most of us attained a certain level of affluence. When the sheer effort to survive exhausts all available resources, families do not worry as much about financial planning. It is when they have a surplus that they begin to plan their decisions.

The so-called Protestant ethic is the foundation of the American Dream. It was expressed classically in Benjamin Franklin's maxims, which generations of Americans have followed religiously: work hard, avoid indulgence, and save for a rainy day. This "Protestant ethic" contributed significantly to our phenomenal economic growth and industrial achievement, whereby until recently about half of all Americans lived in modern postwar houses, 80 percent owned a TV, 75 percent had automatic washing machines, and the number of private automobiles was increasing three times as fast as the population.

The theology of Wesley and Calvin supported this "ethic" to some extent. Calvin emphasized gaining and saving, and saw material success as a sign of God's grace. The link here to the "Protestant ethic" is clear, as is the root of some Americans' negative attitudes toward the poor. Wesley went beyond gaining and saving to emphasize giving as the chief sign of grace. He celebrated fiscal astuteness as instrumental to giving all that you can.

Wesley taught his followers to gain all they could, but not at the expense of life, health, or neighbor; to save all they could, but not to show off or waste or indulge themselves or their children; and then to give all they could as good stewards of all of life. Money was not to be disparaged, by any means. It was an instrument for accomplishing God's purposes.*

The secular ethic lacks this stewardship context. Business forces have been bent on using advertising to convince everyone in affluent America to borrow, spend, waste, and want more. Never have so many owed so much! Americans have lost the thrift focus of the secular ethic, but it would not have remained viable for long anyway. It was far too individualistic. Also, it was based on an economy of scarcity, which rendered it obsolete until the very recent increase in our awareness of the finiteness of the world's resources.

Rethinking Values

With the energy shortage and a raised consciousness concerning world hunger, some persons have begun to rethink their high-consumption life-styles. The church has a major task not only in helping to shape national policy but also in helping families to rethink their values. Many persons today are becoming disillusioned with the American Dream and need help in formulating a new ethic that will embody a global perspective and give high priority to human values and relationships.

Roy Anderson, vice-president of a large insurance corporation, recently told a group involved in family financial planning that he sees America entering a new phase of its history. It is no longer possible to plan for the future simply on the basis of what has happened in the past. We are in a new situation, wherein one must tune in to future trends in order to plan. Anderson thinks we must gear down to a reduced level of affluence. It no longer serves the best interests of society for enterpreneurs to be fostering an ever-increasing desire for consumer products.

The evil is not in money as such, but in our attitudes toward it and in our misuses of it. Money is a social contract. For its value or disvalue one must look to the relationship between the users of the money, the partners to the contract. Our concern is with the nexus of relationships in these social contracts. Can the good of the whole be affirmed by a given contract? The danger is myopia, a narrow focus of concern embodying only the immediate situation.

It is clear that the religious community cannot escape by burying its head in the sand or pretending that it is unconcerned about material things. Religious leaders have been far too squeamish about money, and the spiritual danger is just as great for those who attempt to separate themselves from money concerns as it is for those who embrace them. People who plan at least have opportunity to reflect on and express their own values, whereas the non-planner has little or no chance to do that.

What is needed is a radical reassessment of the goals and basic values that we are consigning to the next generation. The energy crunch and environmental impact studies are pushing us as a society toward such reevaluation. The financial situation today is adding incentives for that process. The New Testament guidelines on stewardship provide a direction for such reevaluation. The church possesses the resources and is in a strategic position to lead the way through its counseling and educational ministries.

2. Counseling in Financial Crises

Harvey and Sue met during their college years. They attended a private college in the East. Sue's family could afford the high costs of her education, while Harvey was able to attend the same school only by virtue of an academic scholarship. He worked part-time as well, and it was always a struggle for him to make ends meet. They were married immediately following their graduation. Harvey enrolled in seminary and Sue attended a nearby university to complete a teacher's certificate. Sue's family helped the couple financially, and Harvey received some financial aid from both the seminary and his denomination. Seminary years were relatively happy for Harvey and Sue. During Harvey's senior year, the couple celebrated the birth of their first child. Sue wanted to have one or two children before launching her teaching career.

Upon completion of seminary, Harvey became pastor of a small congregation. Though Sue's parents were willing to continue helping the young couple, Harvey adamantly opposed further assistance. He had approved of Sue's parents helping them complete their education, but now he wanted to assume full responsibility for their growing family. Sue agreed in principle about their being self-sufficient as a family. However, she had plans for decorating and home furnishing which were elaborate and well beyond their means. This was the beginning of a long story of resentment toward Harvey's chosen vocation. The couple's lack of affluence and Harvey's stubborn insistence that they live on their own income triggered bitter arguments.

Money and Marital Conflict

Conflict in marriage can easily arise as a result of the differing expectations that the spouses bring to the marriage from their diverse socioeconomic backgrounds. Making a new marriage work is difficult enough when the values and life experiences of husband

and wife are similar, but when they are dissimilar, life-style conflicts are compounded. Disagreements arise over many things, including how the family spends for home furnishings, clothing, food, and vacation. But the real issues are often at a deeper level. Behavior that appears to the spouse as showing a lack of support may actually be nothing but the continuation of a life-style now regarded as "normal" because of its having been learned so early in life.

Both spouses, for example, may since childhood have been accustomed to considerable affluence before, as adults, finally entering a lower-paying profession such as the ministry. If so, they will have to do some serious adjusting of their expectations. Even then, it may be tempting for the nonclergy spouse to blame the partner's vocational choice for their family's financial difficulty. The clergy spouse often feels squeezed between the expectations of the congregation on the one hand and those of the parsonage family on the other. Such expectations may be grounded in reality or merely presumed by the minister. Thus clergy can squeeze themselves into a tight box either by trying to meet the assumed expectations or by resisting and resenting them. The only way to untangle the myth from the reality is to open up dialogue with all concerned.

During my parish ministry in northern California we were living in a rented parsonage and the congregation was considering the option to buy or build. As we discussed these possibilities within the committee charged to make the decision, it was enlightening to hear various assumptions emerge. For example, some persons assumed that I would want the parsonage located right next door to the church. The ideas about ministers that some lay persons carry around in their heads are utterly amazing! Ministers' views of lay people are often equally misinformed.

In many cases, neither the minister nor the lay person is rigidly committed to these erroneous ideas and their perpetuation; it's just that the preconceived notions live on until at some point they are finally expelled by fresh information. I found my northern California congregation to be not rigid but flexible, quite open to my ideas once I dared to risk sharing them. After all, most of the existing impressions about ministers were created in people's minds by our predecessors. We can feel free to create alternative or updated impressions.

Incidentally, a church can unwittingly place the clergy family in a bind when housing is purchased with consideration only for the quality of the investment, and little or no sensitivity is shown to the requirements or expectations of the family that will live there. I wholeheartedly support the improvement of standards for church-owned housing, but affluent churches often purchase property in neighborhoods that would otherwise be beyond the financial means of their clergy family. What appears, at first, to be a bonus situation may, at times, turn out to put a great burden on parsonage families when they are pressured to live in a neighborhood style they cannot afford. Pastor and parish need to communicate about these matters.

Spouses too should communicate in order to clarify their current expectations rather than continue living with outdated myths. Where there are real conflicts, compromises can be worked out through negotiation.

Financial Management

One system that inevitably feeds conflict is that in which there is an arbitrary "boss." It is true that in many respects such a style is easier to manage than a system in which the decision making is shared and the power spread around. However, the "boss" style has a high cost. A plan imposed by one spouse or member of a household on another (especially one adult imposing on another adult) tends to increase the sense of isolation of those imposed on, opening the door to resistance and conflict. Domination invites retaliation, sometimes quite overt in nature but sometimes more subtle, such as the withholding of sexual contact, foot-dragging on responsibilities, indifference to goals, or lack of motivation to co-operate. More overt forms of resistance include purchasing unneeded items and encouraging dependence on gifts from relatives as a way of attacking the adequacy of the dominant partner. Sometimes a dominant spouse uses money to control behavior in other areas through punishment and rewards: "You do this for me, and maybe we can afford to eat out tonight."

Unilateral decision-makers tend to avoid planning, or at least putting their plan in writing. Such lack of openness increases fear in the other partner, who never knows where the family stands financially. When told that "we can't afford it," the person has no recourse but to accept the judgment even while doubting its validity. Vagueness and confusion over finances can be used as tools

to manipulate, as can periodic blowups and charges of extrava-
gance.

Manipulative styles of financial management tend to continue
even when a marriage terminates. A couple unable to work out a
mutually satisfying style of financial planning while they are
married find it virtually impossible to separate without fighting
over every piece of furniture, every dollar in the bank, inheritances
from the families of origin, custody and/or visitation rights, and
every other item of mutual concern. One husband in the midst of
getting a divorce actually suggested bidding for every piece of
furniture as a way of determining its monetary value. "It works
fine in the business world," he exclaimed. No-fault divorce has
ended the practice of filing criminal charges in court, but it has not
simplified the settling of financial affairs. If couples are having
power struggles, as many are, these will nearly always surface at
the point where money is concerned. That is why the financial
arena is also such a viable point for potentially constructive intervention—and why financial planning involves much more than
simply making a budget or electing a family treasurer.

The Balance of Power

Another source of marital conflict stems from the impact of
changing roles of women and men today. Much has been written
about the women's movement and all the consequent changes. I
will not elaborate on them here except as they relate to family
financial planning. Where financial planning is done cooperatively
in a climate of trust and openness, the alignment of power is established fairly and acknowledged to be fair. This tends to minimize
conflict and strengthen the relationship. The objective in planning,
then, is to increase the sense of justice or fairness, as well as of
power, for all family members.

The paradox here is apparent. As you eliminate one source of
conflict by moving from a dominant-spouse style of financial planning to a more democratic style, you invite yet another source of
conflict. Every shift of the power balance in the family is accompa-
nied by increased anxiety and usually some overt conflict.

Most families have already experienced major shifts in the balance of power, with a spouse entering a career or taking a part-
time job. The women's movement has facilitated many changes
that will in the long run be beneficial to family life as well as to

the individuals involved. Meanwhile, however, families struggle to understand and assimilate the role and power changes, and to deal with their feelings of fear and resentment as well as anticipation and hope.

Sometimes one almost feels like the little boy who, while standing by his baby sister's crib, looked up wistfully at his father and asked, "Daddy, do you think there will be enough air for all of us to breathe?" As a forty-seven-year-old father of four, with two daughters and a wife in college, that feeling was not unknown to me! And yet I let months go by while I kept all my painful feelings to myself so as not to burden my spouse, who, I assumed, had pressure enough on her after returning to school in her forties. But then digestive problems and some heart palpitations signaled to me that I was not the macho strong-man I thought I was.

It seems that I must relearn this lesson every few years. This past summer has been for me another time of confrontation and renewal. I have been getting in touch with just how vulnerable I am, and becoming more aware of how entrenched I get in work and worry. The mid-years require much energy just trying to survive the pressures of parenting, managing one's career, caring for aging parents, and keeping one's marriage meaningful. Enormous energy is also consumed in wondering how long one can keep the whole show financially solvent.

Counseling in Money Matters

Opportunities for counseling abound in relation to the financial concerns and problems of people. The counseling itself, though, as always, need not be confined to the presenting situation.

The Problem of Job Loss

Can you imagine the immense pain and shock experienced by one who, faced with all the usual problems of family living, is suddenly laid off? Unemployment figures are currently high, especially in some sections of the country. The loss of a job can be a devastating experience. It threatens not only economic security but emotional stability as well. Indeed, loss of employment by the breadwinner can suddenly plunge a harmonious family into chaos.

As we have seen, change of any kind can be a source of stress that leads to conflict. A radical change like that from employment to unemployment often produces loss of self-esteem and security, fear of the future, and in some cases, emotional depression. Job loss is frequently experienced as rejection, with essentially the same hurt being experienced as when one loses a valued friend. Many people also feel a certain social stigma when they are fired. The unemployed person's efforts to cope and to work out powerful feelings may lead to conflict in the family. Loss of employment is a change that requires a total family effort to resolve.

Jake, an active layman in a church I once served as pastor, had his military career cut short by physical disability due to wounds received during the Korean conflict. He was an ambitious career officer. When I met him, Jake was trying to adjust to a second career. He was not coping well. Actually, he spent most of his time at the Officers' Club of a nearby military post, drinking with his buddies. It was not long until Jake's marriage too was in trouble and he was separated from his wife and three small children.

Situations like Jake's often require professional counseling, along with a great deal of support from church, family, and friends. Jake's drinking problem compounded the original problem of a career transition and made the family counseling situation very difficult. I was able to get Jake into an Alcoholics Anonymous group and his wife into an Al-Anon group designed to help the families of problem drinkers. My pastoral focus was largely on Jake's career and family problems. I saw each spouse alone at times but usually worked with them together. Jake had a lot of grief to work through relating to the loss of his cherished military career. Gradually he was able to let go of his former dreams and embrace a new future, even if it involved a second-best career. As Jake's future came alive again, his drinking moderated and the family resumed functioning in a more harmonious manner.

In contrast to the days of the Great Depression, insurance programs today replace some of the wages lost by unemployment. While such programs may prevent total economic disaster, radical financial adjustments are usually necessary by the family experiencing job loss. The major family crisis, however, may be the emotional impact of these changes. The church has a role to play in supporting such a family emotionally as well as in being sensitive to the physical needs.

A church in Minnesota has recently formed a Job Transition Support Group to respond to the need of unemployed persons in their community.* The group has been meeting every other week now for a couple of years. Meetings focus on fellowship and on sharing some specific skills such as job interviewing and résumé writing. The group experience includes a time for prayer and encouragement from Scripture. This is one church's creative way of helping families through a critical time of transition.

Compulsive Spending as Symptom

Most of my counseling experience with families in financial crisis occurred during my years as a counselor to clergy. Fred, a young pastor only a few years out of seminary, was serving his second parish. He told me that he was not satisfied with his ministry and wanted career counseling. So Fred and I began a process of career assessment.

After a few weeks of counseling, as trust developed between us, Fred began to express some other areas of need. His marriage was one area not satisfying him. Finally, he brought out the problem which concerned him most of all: he was head over heels in debt, not for necessities but for expensive hobbies like photography. Rarely could Fred resist a bargain on a camera or a piece of photographic equipment. We spent several more weeks exploring his compulsive buying pattern and its relationship to the other areas of dissatisfaction in his life. It became clear, as time went on, that Fred was attempting to compensate for his failure to work out meaningful relationships in personal and professional life by buying himself expensive presents. This attempted solution was partially satisfying, but as his debts exceeded his ability to meet the payments, the "solution" became a full-blown problem in its own right.

As Fred and I became aware of how his compulsive spending sprees were not an evil, wicked, malicious, or even a sick pattern of behavior so much as an honest attempt to fill a void in his life, he was able to relax a bit. Gradually his guilt subsided too, and he was able to look at the total context of his life in an effort to discover more productive solutions to his problems.

Problem or Symptom?

Fred needed help in financial planning to stabilize his family's financial situation, but that alone would have been only a temporary solution. Financial institutions say that 80% of the families they help out of financial difficulty are right back in trouble within two years. Thus it is necessary to get beyond the symptom to the underlying problem in these families' lives. Once they understand their compulsive spending patterns as an attempted solution to emotional and interpersonal problems, they are in a better position to seek a change in their patterns of relating—a much more profound level of change. In the case of Fred, we brought his wife Jane into our counseling so they could work together on their relationship. In the long run, Fred and Jane solved a lot more than simply a financial problem in their family.

Family therapists have learned from experience with many family systems that although families do their best to cope with their environment and to work out solutions to their problems, sometimes those "solutions" pose a bigger problem than the one they were designed to solve. In such instances, the focus for intervention needs to be on the attempted solution rather than on the presenting problem.

For some clergy families I have counseled, the problem was essentially financial. Their focus on money was not merely symptomatic.

John and Pat were serving a cluster of rural churches. John drove more than 50,000 miles a year ministering to his expansive parish. Even prior to the skyrocketing escalation of gas prices, John's annual fuel costs were phenomenal. Furthermore, he wore out a car in less time than he could afford to pay for it. Heating for the large old frame parsonage cost two or three times that of a modern ranch home in the city. John's salary was barely above the minimum level, and he and Pat had three children. Clearly, this family had a financial problem.

Our counseling was an effort to explore the various options open to them for negotiating a change in their situation. One of the options explored was for John and Pat to inform judicatory executives about their family's plight. We also discussed how John and Pat could share their situation openly with the appropriate lay committees in their parish.

Many ministers assume that persons in their parish are aware of their problems and either do not care or are powerless to help. In most cases this is untrue. We all have an amazing ability to misread the situations of others or to assume that as long as they do not complain things must be OK. The only way to break this stalemate is to take the risk of informing the appropriate persons about our situation and trust that they will respond in caring ways.

Most ministers I have spoken with are reluctant to complain, because they know the church budget is tight and they feel guilty about requesting a larger share of it for their own use. Then, as their families suffer, these ministers feel additional guilt about not having provided adequately. Thus, the minister gets locked into a vicious cycle.

Most of the persons with whom I have counseled about financial problems have, like Fred and Jane, additional or underlying personal or family problems related to the financial crisis. This is not to say that clergy salaries are usually adequate, but only that most clergy and their middle-class laity, like John and Pat, suffer less from too few resources than from a lack of planning in a situation that may be further complicated with role-change struggles, value conflicts, and the normal crises attendant upon moving into new stages of the family life cycle. Pastoral counselors need to sharpen their diagnostic skills in order to discern when the problem is essentially a financial one and when money is merely symptomatic of other kinds of struggles.

Diagnostic Clues

In order to do improved diagnosis in counseling, you need to take time to listen carefully and watch for certain clues. Look for any recent changes in the environment of the family: a move, a job change, a divorce, a death in the extended family, children leaving home, birth of a child, a promotion, or a role change perhaps attendant upon one spouse taking a new job. Any of these changes can upset both the emotional and fiscal balance of the family. Significant change in the way a family handles its finances can be an early warning sign of a disturbance in the power structure of the family. Fred's impulsive spending pattern illustrates this dynamic. He was attempting to regain through budgetary excesses the sense of control he no longer experienced in his profession or in his marriage.

In the financial arena an additional clue is to be found in the very use or nonuse of a family financial plan. Are goals understood by all family members? Is there a budget? Who makes the financial decisions? Are there signs of manipulation through punishment or rewards? Is there any resistance and foot-dragging by one spouse or the other? All of these can be signals of underlying relational dynamics.

Referral

If the problem is primarily a financial one—that is, if there is generally an absence of the clues listed above—then you may elect to refer your counselee to an appropriate fiscal resource person who possesses the needed expertise. Budget counseling, for example, may be the only help needed if a single person or family, generally adequate in personality and management skills, is temporarily overwhelmed by debts that have accrued because of external pressures such as unanticipated medical costs, educational expenses, or temporary work stoppage. If on the other hand a value conflict is involved, who is better equipped to help than the pastor?

If the problem involves family relationships, a trained specialist in pastoral counseling may be an appropriate resource for the family. Or if as pastor you do not have the time to work with the family, or the problem is too complex, then referral to a trained pastoral counselor or a marriage and family counselor would be appropriate.* Your role in this instance would be one of diagnosis and referral.

Chapters 5 and 6 will be helpful in identifying community resources that may be helpful in both financial counseling and educational ventures.

Families and Finances

A particularly difficult area of family financial counseling involves living arrangements and/or care of elderly family members. Often neither older persons nor their children possess sufficient funds to provide for living apart from one another. Adult children may hesitate to arrange for separate living quarters, such as a retirement home, because of their feelings of guilt about putting a parent away or their fear of incurring a parent's wrath, even though such an arrangement might be best for all concerned.

It is usually best to approach such sticky situations by confronting them openly along with everyone involved, including the older persons, whose lives may literally be at stake in such decisions. Moving from one location to another is stressful for any of us at any age, but even more so in later years. Friends, personal possessions, familiar surroundings, and the routines to which we have become accustomed are all a very important part of life's meaning. They all help us to maintain orientation of life and interest in living. To lose any or all of these suddenly, and with no opportunity to participate in the decision making, causes us to feel impotent, invites resistance and anger, and leaves us grieving without resources for coping. No wonder so many older persons die soon after being moved from one setting into another. Many families require pastoral care, including financial counseling, during these difficult transition periods.

Counseling on financial issues with single parents often includes help beyond financial management. The opportunity may arise to facilitate unfinished grief work, anger, guilt, depression—issues that affect not only the single parent but the children as well. Gifts lavished on children by divorced parents may communicate to those children that the tragedy of divorce grants them permission to become exploitative. Similarly, overindulgence on the part of a divorced parent in the matter of allowances, privileges, or gifts may be a form of bribery and/or competition for the affection of the children. These excuses are a common focus of counseling with single parents.

Single persons without children may also be in need of financial counseling. I recall a newspaper feature bearing the headline: "She's 33, single, pregnant, and in debt for $24,000." Jean Evans apparently took her problems to the Consumer Credit Counselors of her city: she had expenses of $692 a month, income of $634 a month, and a baby on the way. "I finally came here," she said, "because my creditors are bugging me and threatening to turn my account over to an attorney if I do not pay, and I can't."

Jean's financial problem had started after her divorce some five years earlier. At that time, she made a job change involving a cut in salary. Her expenses were fixed—food, rent, clothing, and a car—not much to cut down on. "My apartment costs $225 and I cannot find anything cheaper. I am looking for a roommate. It seems like living alone and having a car you cannot save anything."

Children and the Culture

Most young persons today have grown up with some measure of affluence yet at a considerable distance from the economic sources of that affluence. Children today are usually not as close to the family source of income (the farm or small business) as in earlier generations, nor are they involved in the financial operations or decision-making processes of the family. They really do not know what their parents do, where the money comes from, what it means to the family, or how the financial decisions are made.

In addition to being unfamiliar with family financial issues, many young persons today have a feeling of entitlement when it comes to money and the things money can buy. It seems to many of them that money is just there and that they should have their due share. Many get it through intrafamily transfers. Some economists refer to the 300 billion dollars transferred by inheritance each year as "heir pollution." People who are not on the receiving end of an inheritance may attempt to achieve their expectations through the use of credit. The result is a large number of single young adults who are deeply in debt trying to realize their dreams right now.

Obviously, you cannot easily change the cultural milieu in which your children grow up, but you can make an effort to communicate a different set of values—not by words alone but by what you demonstrate with your life-style. I have no doubt that I have been brainwashed with the American Dream and so caught up in it that I have contributed significantly to my children's attitudes about money and possessions. I have done this through my choice of neighborhoods (when I have had a choice), my spending habits, my style-conscious clothing purchases, and my impulse buying. My mid-life reevaluation time has revealed just how oppressive possessions can become—just to maintain and replace and worry about them.

Many people today are becoming disillusioned with the American Dream and its inherent consumer psychology of "just a little bit more." This new feeling opens the door for a process of values transformation, reassessment of goals, and the establishment of a new direction for the individuals and families with whom you counsel. Your knowledge of financial planning will enable you to help many of these people, thereby strengthening your total counseling ministry.

3. The Financial Plan

There is a scene in Aristophanes' "The Clouds" in which a troubled individual consults Socrates about his anxiety and insomnia. The man is told to lie on a couch and speak freely concerning the problem. He speaks of the moon and his fantasy of capturing it and putting it in his pocket, thereby preventing it from waxing and waning; obviously, the first of the month never comes! Aristophanes was of course writing about a different set of problems, but the symptom is familiar and has been around for quite some time: payday never comes, at least not in sufficient strength or numbers.

You may have thought that financial planning was only for the affluent, or the very poor. Though helpful to everyone, such planning is especially important to those in the middle-income range, who this year have barely enough money to buy a new car, or carpet the living room, or take the family vacation trip. The affluent can do all three. The poor have a hard time doing any of these things because they can manage little more than basic survival needs and do not have access to credit. The middle-income group worries less about sheer survival, has easy credit, and is therefore most vulnerable to the pressures of consumerism and commercial advertising.

Most clergy can benefit from financial planning, not merely to avoid catastrophe but also to be certain that their true values are reflected in their living. The vast majority of lay persons to whom clergy minister are likewise in need of financial planning. This chapter describes in detail the ingredients of a typical financial plan, and follows one individual and one family through the life cycle to show how planning is a changing and ongoing process. It should help you begin, or carry forward more effectively, your own financial planning. It should also give you the background to help troubled individuals or families in counseling and to develop educational programs for various groups.

Planning and the Life Cycle

Planning involves a process. It is not a "once done" act but something to be continued through all of life. Life proceeds through stages, each stage introducing a new set of tasks and responsibilities. A sound financial plan based on anticipated change-points during the life cycle will help to bring added stability and solidarity to single persons as well as to family units.

The chart below illustrates some probable change-points in the "traditional family" life cycle. This illustration, of course, does not apply to all families. Every family, however structured, must identify its own unique change-points and plan accordingly. A more elaborate chart of the family life cycle, including personal role changes, family structure changes, and dominant family and environmental forces, is given in appendix A.

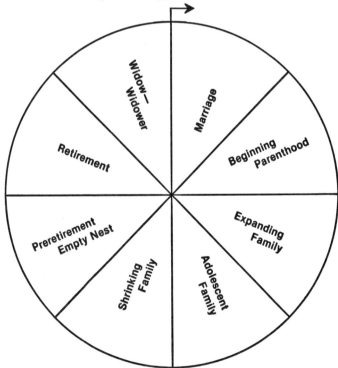

During childhood, the individual's financial needs are usually met by the parents. Eight-year-old Sally has little understanding of the marketplace through which her needs are met. To be prepared for adulthood she must learn about stores, money, ownership, purchase transactions, and skills in choosing among alternatives. During childhood Sally is vulnerable to the media onslaught which creates desire for products of all kinds; she thinks she should have everything she sees on television.

As Sally grows into adolescence she begins to develop more individual taste, though she remains susceptible to peer pressure. Sally and her friends tend to be conscious of name brands. That little label on the back pocket of their jeans makes all the difference in the world. If Sally's peers are wearing a certain brand of jeans or shoes, no other brand, even if it is of equal or superior quality, will do. It is important for Sally to learn such marketplace concepts as price/quality relationship, comparison shopping, impulse buying, and decision making. Typically she and her friends have problems with identifying product differences and with understanding the value of money in relation to their tastes and preferences. Some teenagers are tempted to cut corners dangerously by shoplifting and/or using such illegal products as drugs or alcohol.

As Sally becomes a young adult she struggles with unclear values. Her age group is highly mobile, has few financial burdens or assets, and is even more conscious of fashions. Sally is talking about having her own car. She has a stereo and lots of sports equipment, and is constantly on the go with her friends. They are into all sorts of entertainment, including concerts, records, and eating out. Sally has begun to use credit, when her parents permit her to use their plastic cards. Sally and her parents are beginning to talk together about the merits of budgeting, renting versus owning, and credit.

Sally moves into mature singlehood as she graduates from college and gets her first full-time job. She begins to make commitments to a life-style, and to think seriously about career. Many young adults today are staying in the single category longer, postponing marriage. They may share housing with other singles (often in committed relationships) or live alone. Inflation is forcing more and more unmarried young adults to share housing. Sally now has more money to spend as she wants, and she has more knowledge about products. Sally shares an apartment with a girl friend. They are interested in purchasing some expensive furnishings and appliances. They enjoy travel and dining in the better restaurants, and make many hobby-related purchases. Financial planning could be useful to Sally and her age group, if knowledge of this planning were readily accessible to them. They would profit from familiarity with tax shelters, investments, and inflation. Some issues they face include financial support and help with household tasks during illness, inappropriate package sizes, and considerations of owning versus renting.

Sally has been dating Joe since college days. Joe has been moving up in his engineering firm for a couple of years now, so they decide to get married. Young marrieds with no children are usually better off financially than they will be later should they decide to have children. The major issue for newly married Sally and Joe is that of working out their value differences and learning how to make joint decisions. Many of their arguments reflect their diverse expectations with respect to money in marriage. Joe is concerned about long-range planning, whereas Sally has become accustomed to spending for the things she wants today. Sally is interested in household furnishings, a car, travel, clothing, and entertainment. Joe insists that they should be saving for the purchase of a home of their own. He does not want to live in an apartment forever. They both recognize the need to protect their assets with insurance.

Joe and Sally need help with values clarification, goal setting, budget planning, and learning to keep records of expenditures for tax purposes and for future planning. They are vulnerable to impulse buying and tend to live only for the present. Learning to plan ahead and to set aside a portion of their funds for future use will make the transition into the next phase of their lives considerably easier. Fortunately for Joe and Sally, their church includes in its marriage enrichment seminars a section on financial planning.

A few years later Joe and Sally have two small children. With the arrival of children, their financial situation and life-style change drastically. Sally, no longer working outside the home, is bringing in no income. Young marrieds with children have more financial obligations and, in most cases, less discretionary money. Couples who do not plan ahead for this eventuality experience increased stress in their relationship as a result of this financial turnaround. If the decision to begin a family is not a mutual one, the situation may be further complicated by hostility or resentment. Sally and Joe have most of the concerns of young singles and, in addition, the expenses related to child-rearing, such as clothing, toys, educational expenses, a mortgage on the new house, and a larger car.

Growing young families should learn about real estate, taxes, loans, estate planning, wills, and trusts. They also have the task of helping their children to develop and apply values and to be discriminating in purchases. Typical problems are credit abuse, underestimated costs of raising children in an inflationary period, finding reliable maintenance and repair services for the home and car, and finding appropriate health-care services for the family.

As the children grow older the homemaking spouse may return to a career or initiate a new one, return to school to prepare for a career, or take a part-time job. Depending on the plan followed, such a career change may either add to the family income or become an additional expense. As Sally returns to her old job the financial pressure eases a bit. Joe and Sally are tempted again to live for the present only and to use all available funds for moving into a bigger house and buying a second car. For other families in this situation, the temptation may be to buy more labor-saving gadgets, a recreation vehicle, a boat, or other luxuries for leisure-time amusement. Many of these items can and do enhance family life, but if attention is not devoted to planning for the next phase of the family life cycle, another shock will hit when the children are ready for college.

Joe and Sally forego the larger house, but they do buy a second car. They also begin a college fund for the kids. The last few years before children leave the family nest (usually mid-career for parents) can be another financially difficult time. In addition to the expenses associated with launching children into college, marriage, or work, there are often costs related to the care of aging parents. Even though most mid-years adults are at or near their peak earning power, the fiscal stress of this period is unusually high. Food costs, clothing, medical and dental expenses all seem to peak during this stage. All those appliances and leisure products now need maintenance and/or replacement. Along with the marketplace sophistication gained from earlier experience and from the church's marriage enrichment seminar, Joe and Sally now need information on college costs, tax shelters, nursing homes, and funeral arrangements. The ongoing marrieds group at their church is planning to bring in some community resource persons to talk about these topics.

Some couples require counseling to assist them in preparing for the empty nest. Helping children with choices of college, career, or marriage is only part of what occurs during this life stage. Sally and Joe are beginning to think about their own retirement. They realize that it is not too early to begin planning ahead for that stage of the life cycle. Among other major expenses in the mid-years are inflation, transportation for all family members, and automobile insurance for teenage dependents. This period is also an important one for the continuing education of young people in finance and values clarification.

If a mid-years family has experienced marital separation or divorce, the economic pressure may be even heavier. Financial costs are usually higher for a separated or divorced family than for one which stays together. The expenses of two homes, alimony, child support, and added travel expenses are likely to push the combined outlays for two households to at least 50 percent more than for one. Add the costs of legal fees, and one realizes that divorce, especially where children are involved, can be a costly mid-life burden.

Once the children are launched, Sally and Joe expect about fifteen years together before retirement. This period has been lengthened in recent times by the combination of smaller families and a longer life expectancy. As Joe's and Sally's income and expenses level off, the family's economic picture stabilizes and marital tensions decrease. However, for some families, the effect can be just the reverse. Loss of the gratification provided by children and loss of the children as a buffer, absorbing some of the emotional and physical energies of the parents, can stimulate new money problems or aggravate old ones. Some people find fault with how the spouse spends or manages money—because it seems easier to argue about money than to discuss sexual needs or other areas of pain between them. For most couples, including Joe and Sally, the empty-nest period is a more peaceful one, characterized by freedom from the anxieties and pressures of child-rearing. The relationship between Joe and Sally takes on a new level of companionship and sharing. The training and fellowship opportunities provided by their church have helped prepare them to make the most of this period.

Like most older middle-class married couples who no longer have dependents at home, Joe and Sally own their home. Their financial position is stronger than ever. New products are of less interest. Occasional financial aid is offered to children and to aging parents as a matter of choice or of necessity. Expenses include more travel, self-improvement classes, and hobby-related purchases. Joe and Sally are now saving substantial sums for retirement.

The life-style of Joe and Sally will not fit the value choices of every family. I describe it here only to show how clear and solid planning assisted them in successfully launching their children and in reaching a happy and fruitful retirement period. Research shows that only 27 percent of senior citizens are "enjoyers" like Sally and Joe, managing to cope well with the aging process. Another 53 percent are "survivors," coping adequately with most problems but poorly with some. The remaining 20 percent are the casualties, "crushed by the difficulties of aging." About 70 percent of all persons in this period of the life cycle, both married and single, report that inflation depresses them psychologically.*

Retired singles, including those divorced or widowed, may suffer drastic decreases in income. Mass transportation becomes a major necessity. Medical care and health-related products are increasingly important. Knowledge of Medicare, Social Security, community resources, wills and trusts, and estate planning are required. These persons need information about nutrition and skills in keeping records for government transfer payment programs like Social Security and Medicare. Such persons are often vulnerable to exploitation by door-to-door salespersons. They may need physical support during an illness. They often need help in understanding age-related difficulties such as the use of hearing aids.

Single parents compose another group which has a special set of needs for financial planning and counseling. They face most of the problems of two-parent families, but without benefit of the skills, knowledge, income, time, and energy of a partner. They may try to compensate for these missing assets themselves, or perhaps buy them. Single parents are often heavy users of housekeeping and day-care services, and they may do more purchasing of recreational opportunities for their children. They may need education to prepare for entry or reentry into the job market. Their legal expenses may also be unusually high. Single-parent families actually require more money, but usually have less.

What I have attempted to illustrate is that families, like individuals, pass through a cycle of fiscal growth and change. Two individuals enter marriage from different backgrounds, with varying sets of expectations, attitudes, and experiences. They bring all this to their new family system, which exists in a money world. This necessitates a lot of communication, adjustment, compromise —all part of the planning for their new shared lives.

We have seen that expenses tend to increase steadily until children are launched. Then an economic plateau is attained, where parents have an opportunity to plan for their retirement years. At different stages of the life cycle, individuals and families have different needs, wants, and values. Unexpected contingencies like major illness, divorce, or the death of a spouse can impose great stress on the family system, along with heavy financial obligations. Some of these unexpected contingencies need to be provided for, along with the expected changes which occur routinely from one stage of the life cycle to the next.

Characteristics of Financial Planning

Several important characteristics of financial planning emerge from this discussion of family dynamics and the life cycle. Five are particularly worth noting.

First, the process should be intentional, since planning does not happen unless we make it happen. The clergy families I have spoken with are always hopeful that "things will work out," but few are intentional in their planning efforts. At best they look a few months ahead, while most just drift along from month to month.

Second, the process is value-based. The place for the family to start is not with a budget but with dialogue concerning the family's purpose and direction. What is your family all about? What do you want to accomplish in your particular family? What qualities do you want to reflect in your style of living? What are your needs as distinguished from your wants? Luxuries for one family may be necessities for another. You should understand whether you are using your money to buy things and services or states of mind, like "keeping up with the Joneses." Economic behavior is determined by your values and priorities. Values and priorities must be clarified and organized by the changing family at each phase of the life cycle.

Third, the process of financial planning is goal-oriented. Following the clarification of priorities based on needs and values, you should set some goals that can serve as a chart for your course. Some goals may be long-range in nature, while others may be short-term. It is important to describe them in concrete terms. These goals will help you know what to start doing now, and six months from now, in order to make your plan operational.

Fourth, financial planning is a time-phased process. Financial planning is inextricably tied to the biological clock. This gives us a structure for planning ahead to the next stage. Not many families will plan very far ahead, but at least you can be aware of the life-cycle process and plan at least one stage in advance.

Finally, financial planning is futuristic. This does not mean that you live constantly for tomorrow. On the contrary, planning enables you to enjoy today because you took a little time yesterday to think ahead. You may recall how such planning helped Joe and Sally move smoothly from one stage of their lives to the next. Instead of always being surprised and caught short, with every life-cycle transition plunging them into a new crisis, they lived in a generally smooth, comfortable manner, because they anticipated change and provided for future needs. This permitted them to maintain control of their lives rather than trusting entirely to chance.

Steps in Financial Planning

To help organize the planning process with your own family or that of a parishioner, think in terms of a logical sequence of considerations. Four major steps can make up the process.

Goals

First, through family dialogue, your family's values and needs are clarified, and some goals for your stage of the life cycle are established. These emerging goals will give you some idea of the demands or requirements placed upon your resources for the immediate period as well as for the years ahead.

Some of your goals will not be money-related at all, but may be time-related and/or energy-related. Though most persons, when financial planning is mentioned, think immediately of budgeting, budget is only one dimension of financial planning.

Resources

Second, before you develop a spending plan, you need to assess your resources. Employment is the major source of money, but some families also receive money from interest on savings, return on investments, real-estate rentals, bequests, pension, Social Security, and gifts. Credit is another source of money; when used with discretion it can be a valuable asset at various points in the life cycle. Added to money are all the human strengths and abilities of the family: talents, time, creative energy. Together, these make up the family's total resources, in light of which the plan for utilization can be made.

If you think only in terms of cash salary or take-home pay in your assessment, you may underestimate your creative possibilities for responding to the family's needs and goals. A total assessment of resources can open the way for the family to find new ways to meet changing needs, including but not limited to obtaining financial resources.

Budget

Third, with a clear statement of goals and a comprehensive assessment of resources in hand, you are ready to begin developing a plan for using your resources to meet your goals. A spending plan, or budget as it is often called, includes costs that recur monthly, quarterly, semiannually, and yearly. Such items as rent or mortgage payments, insurance, taxes, charitable contributions, and utilities are relatively fixed. Other costs are more variable, though there should always be a place in the budget for them; clothing and food fall into this category of variable expenditures. There are other things that are more optional than food and clothing and thus require even greater flexibility in your planning. Such items may include travel, education, entertainment, and transportation.

How much you spend on these several categories varies at different periods of the life cycle. For example, statistics show that families tend to spend a larger percentage of their budget on clothing when parents are in the 35–44 year age span, more on housing in the younger years, and more on health care in the later years.*

Budgeting involves a plan not only for spending money but also for using other resources like time, talent, skills, and energy. Budgeting means the implementation of your values. It is an effort to put values into operation in an intentional manner. Planning will help you discover the widest and most creative use of your resources.

The budget or spending plan should include: (1) operating expenses—those recurring items that keep the family going from day to day; (2) reserves—those anticipated short-term and irregular expenses which are best provided for through maintaining a reserve (savings, usually) rather than simply hoping that somehow the money will be available when needed for maintenance or possible replacement of home, car, and appliances, or perhaps vacation or medical and dental care, and (3) future capital—the longer-term goals such as purchase of a home, college education, and retirement. Operating expenses and reserves obviously stand higher on the priority list for the family's available resources but, when possible, some commitment should be made to future capital. Sample forms to assist in your planning are included in appendixes B and C.

Protection

Along with assessing resources and developing a plan for the use of these resources in the context of goals and values, thought should be given finally to protecting the financial resources of the family. The family's resources may be threatened by such contingencies as the death of a spouse, physical disability, accident, illness, or other emergency. Insurance is the most common way of protecting our financial resources against unanticipated demands. Upgrading vocational skills and gaining or maintaining accreditation in a profession are also ways of protecting a family's financial security. The need for protection varies in amount and kind from stage to stage of the life cycle but tends to be most acute in the early stages of the family's life, especially where there are children.

A Conceptual Framework

The diagram below illustrates how these basic steps in financial planning are integrated into a comprehensive planning scheme. Goals, resources, budget, and protection are plotted on a grid that relates them to the three categories of funds that make up any spending plan. The diagram may have to be enlarged when it comes to actually filling in the appropriate spaces. The whole matter of resources, including remuneration as well as the use of credit and insurance, will be discussed in greater depth in the next chapter.*

A Comprehensive Planning Scheme

	Operating Expenses	Reserves	Future Capital
Goals			
Resources			
Budget			
Protection			

Remember, your planning process should be flexible. It is your servant, not your master. Planning should not frustrate or discourage you, or become overly time-consuming. It is a tool, and as such will help you avoid impulse buying and move intentionally toward your goals. If your resource assessment and your spending plan are not in balance, you can make the necessary adjustments and thereby avoid problems.

To make any plan work, you must keep records. A sample form is included in appendix D. Basically you need to keep a simple record of what you spend on the various categories in your budget each month. This will let you know whether the plan is working and where you need to modify it. It will also greatly simplify your preparation of income-tax forms at the end of the year. I strongly recommend that you keep a fairly detailed accounting of expenses for at least thirty days to help you discover some of the leaks in your spending habits.

Involving the Children

There seems to be more family communication about money and values today than ever before. Most clergy couples I have spoken with report that they are moving away from a system where one spouse does most of the financial planning, toward one where the decision making is shared. This seems to parallel the trend toward more spouses working outside the home and contributing directly to the family's income. (Homemakers have always contributed indirectly!) These clergy families, however, rarely involve the children in the financial planning. One couple told me that their children "just assume things will always get paid for and money will always be there for whatever they need." The parents who protect their children from financial realities are often those who have no financial plan themselves. Their philosophy is: "If you need it, get it." They have an intuitive sense about not spending more than they receive, but they set no goals for the future other than the hope of someday owning their own home.

José and María are parents in a three-generation household, in which parents and grandparents share in the financial planning but the children are rarely involved. Most of the planning is done by the parents. Since moving to this country from Cuba, María has worked outside the home to help make ends meet. The grandparents also contribute to the food budget. Having the grandparents live in the family home is not a financial burden; indeed, their presence gives their children "peace of mind" and provides for the grandchildren a richer variety of adult role models. The major goal of the parents is to avoid debt. "There is enough stress in the minister's life," explains José, "without adding to it the stress of debt." He remarked that he had learned as a child to turn off the lights when leaving a room—to save money. "Today, this habit conserves energy as well. We try to teach our children this kind of thing."

Whether intentionally or not, children are always learning about the values of their parents through observation. Parents, however, are often reluctant to involve children in discussions of family income and spending. They may wish to protect their children from worry by not involving them in family decision making, but this practice can serve to protect the parents as well, especially if they fear that children will reveal to neighbors a sensitive and private area of their lives. If the values and disvalues of involving children are weighed carefully, however, most parents are likely to come out in favor of their children's participation, at least to some degree, in designing and implementing the family financial plan.

The benefits to the children in thus learning about financial responsibility and management cannot be overestimated. Children are not born with innate values or with skills for managing their resources. They learn by what they see, hear, and experience. Gradually, they will learn the meaning of money and the reasons for spending, saving, and sharing it. They will also learn where it comes from as the family talks about income in relation to work and as they themselves receive an allowance or earn pay for doing odd jobs.

Most teens are eager to earn money and even more ready to spend it. If they have had some experience with family financial planning, they are more likely to think about longer-range plans for spending, saving, and sharing. With some help teens can manage checking and savings accounts and begin to do some budgeting of their own. For teenagers it is important that parents guide rather than direct or dictate.

With children of all ages it is not wise to use money as a reward or punishment. Even though they may be motivated by this approach, such usage unfortunately teaches children how money can be used to manipulate others. We should give them many opportunities to gain experience with money by choosing among alternatives, shopping with parents, handling their own cash, making purchases, sharing money with friends, and contributing to charitable causes. Doing routine family chores without pay helps children gain a sense of ownership and participation in family responsibility.

As children get older an allowance is a useful vehicle for teaching them to handle money. Teens might receive a sufficient amount to cover weekly incidentals such as school lunches and entertainment, and perhaps routine clothing needs. It is helpful to involve the children in decisions regarding allowances, giving them as little supervision as possible so that they can learn from experience.

Parents should also encourage teens to save toward longer-range goals. Sometimes this is best done by example. Parents who themselves put money aside for long-range family goals help adolescents to see the value of the practice. Young people also require help in understanding the relation between the proportions of family income that are used for spending, saving, protection, investing, and sharing. They can learn these things during family planning sessions, along with the purposes, services, and charges of banks, and something about credit and charge accounts. Experience in family planning sessions will help teens in distinguishing between their needs and their wants. They can learn that resources have limits, and they can become familiar with the many channels through which family resources flow to provide food, shelter, heat, light, transportation, clothing, and all the other things they enjoy and use daily. Youngsters tend to take all this for granted until they see a list of categories included in the family budget.

Planning, then, is more than a financial numbers game. It can be positively educational for the children.* It means practice in communication, conflict management, and decision making. It affords experience in values clarification and revision. It requires teamwork and morale building. And it engenders self-respect for each member of the household.

The Inventory of Family Resources chart in appendix E is one I have used in family-life conferences. It provides a useful way for families to begin to assess their current use of resources in several areas. It can be modified and adapted to different family models, but essentially it is designed to give each member of the household a tool for feeding back to the family his or her impression of how other members of the household use their time and money. It helps to open discussion and facilitate talk about basic values for the family.

Some guidelines for group discussion and planning sessions include: (1) encourage participation by all—sharing feelings as well as ideas; (2) avoid judging or analyzing ideas and feelings; (3) create a relaxed and informal atmosphere; (4) assign responsibility to everyone; (5) help the communication process by clarifying what is being said; (6) be patient when an impasse is experienced —talk it through; (7) parents, try always to be good models, as children will be watching and copying you, and finally (8) do not get discouraged when you fail and the process disintegrates—keep trying!

Involvement of the whole family is important in financial planning. It is a means to enhanced family solidarity and stability. It is also good preparation for children and youth, who are likely to face even greater financial difficulty in the years ahead.

4. Financial Planning for Clergy

We come now to discuss fiscal issues that have particular relevance to the clergy family while also being applicable in many ways to families in general. Clergy who can handle financial matters directly affecting themselves are often better equipped to help other people with reference to their financial concerns and problems.

Remuneration

Remuneration of clergy is steadily improving, but most religious leaders would probably agree that it is still inadequate. Clergy families I have talked to are reluctant to sound like complainers; they feel too much commitment to their work. Dora, a pastor's spouse, expressed it this way: "We tithe, and the Lord always takes care of us." Dora revealed, however, that her own mother had had to move out of church-owned housing after her preacher-husband died, and as a widow was totally unprepared to take care of herself. Clergy housing allowances rarely meet actual rent or mortgage payments, and many churches are having an increasingly hard time putting together a financial package that will attract the qualified pastor they desire.

Stewardship Principles

Most clergy think of stewardship in terms of sharing, but how many of us apply the notion of sharing to the matter of obtaining financial resources? What kind of job do clergy do in helping religious institutions apply stewardship principles to the matter of providing adequately for their pastoral leadership? Stewardship has to do not only with individuals' sharing with the church but also with the church's sharing with its pastor—including the provision of fair and appropriate remuneration.

Some religious professionals may themselves be more to blame for their inadequate remuneration than are their congregations. At the core of the problem is the clergy's personal confusion about the value of a pastor's services. This confusion may derive from inadequate focus on a theology of money. The good steward is concerned with everyone's getting a fair shake, including the pastor and the pastor's family. Fairness is not only an economic principle. It is also a spiritual principle, rooted in the scriptural concept of justice. As applied to the cost of pastoral services, it means that institutions paying clergy have a responsibility to plan carefully, pay adequately, and provide for necessary professional expenses so that pastors do not have to cover the costs of doing ministry out of their own compensation. The church is demeaned and ministry weakened when ministers have to struggle to meet basic living expenses. In a land of abundance this is inexcusable.

The congregation's ability to pay for pastoral services is linked directly to its practice of stewardship. It would require only ten tithing families or individuals in a congregation to maintain the minister's income at the average level of these same ten persons or families. Most congregations come nowhere close to their stewardship potential in this regard. It staggers the imagination to think of the potential of twenty, thirty, or even a hundred families committed to the goal of tithing. Most congregations fall short of reaching even half that stewardship goal in terms of total giving.

I know how difficult it is for churches to keep up with inflation. However, many congregations that have the ability to pay their minister fairly simply lack the stewardship commitment to do so. In such instances it would be helpful to make an agreement between pastor and parish as to what mathematically specifiable portion of fair salary can be paid. This raises the congregation's consciousness concerning what fair compensation actually is and how far short of the goal they are. The agreement should include a commitment to promote stewardship and to increase compensation steadily and significantly until fair compensation is achieved. Too often we accept whatever the congregation's finance committee thinks it can pay—or is used to paying—without even raising the issue of whether that is adequate or fair compensation.

How do you arrive at a fair compensation figure? First of all, make a clear distinction between compensation and the expenses of ministering.

Expenses of Ministry

Expenses associated with pastoral service belong to the congregation. These are business expenses and should be in the budget under administrative costs, not under minister's compensation. Such items include supplies, transportation, hospitality costs, continuing improvement of ministerial skills, and an allowance for books and periodicals.

A car allowance, for example, is definitely not part of the minister's salary. It is reimbursement for professional expenses. The ideal arrangement for getting full reimbursement for professional travel would be for the church to own the car you use. The church might choose to lease rather than own, but in either event it would cover all expenses related to that car, including insurance, maintenance, and gas. If you own the car you use for professional travel, it is best to have the church pay you a specified amount-per-mile, based on what it actually costs you to operate your car, including replacement costs. In time of inflation this amount will need to be increased annually. A figure based on mileage should come very close to covering your business expense associated with travel. A less desirable formula is a fixed annual amount to be paid monthly. This method is usually based on an estimate of expenses, and may or may not cover actual costs. (If you spend less than the amount paid, the balance must be considered as income for tax purposes; if you spend more, the excess can be deducted, assuming you have kept adequate records.)

Compensation

Compensation includes salary and benefits only. Salary may include a housing allowance if you are scheduled to receive one.

Housing Allowance

Taxwise, it is advantageous for you to receive a designated housing allowance even if you live in church-owned housing. This is especially true if you pay for any costs related to the maintenance, furnishing, or upkeep of that home. An amount appropriate to your out-of-pocket expenses for the home can be included in such an allowance and excluded from your gross income for tax purposes. If you are buying or renting a home, an appropriately larger amount of compensation should be designated as housing allowance. Whatever expense you incur for providing a home should be covered by a housing allowance, including any mortgage payments, insurance, taxes, maintenance, furnishings, and yard care.

If you live in church-owned housing, you are, in effect, paying rent. A fair rental value would need to be placed on that housing. If you are allowed to choose your own housing, the full allowance should be paid in cash and should be adequate to cover your actual costs.

Benefits

The benefits portion of any compensation package includes retirement or pension plans, life insurance, hospital and disability insurance, and possibly a Social Security allowance. There are tax advantages to having these benefits paid directly by the congregation; the amounts involved are not considered income.

The federal self-employment (Social Security) tax is an exception to this principle. By law the institution is not allowed to pay your self-employment tax. If your congregation pays you a self-employment tax allowance, you must report that amount as income. However, it is still advantageous for you to have the church commit itself to covering this item, because Social Security keeps increasing in cost. Thus with each tax increase you automatically receive an increase in compensation which you would not have otherwise.

Salary

Having clarified what constitutes compensation, we can look at the question of a reasonable salary. To put this in perspective we need to be aware of just how seriously inflation has eroded the value of the dollar. In less than a decade the Consumer Price Index has more than doubled. This means that the cost of living has more than doubled over that same period of time. Recall, for example, what you paid for a movie, a hamburger, a gallon of gasoline, and your first car when you started college. Then think what these things cost today!

You also need to do a little comparing with some other professions—doctors? lawyers? . . . well, maybe public school teachers and administrators. Find out what a teacher with two years of graduate school and eight years of experience will earn in your area on a ten-month contract, and what principals in the same district are paid. Urban public school teachers' salaries, as well as those of government employees generally, have about doubled in the last decade. Firefighter and police officer salaries have more than doubled in that same period. How about your salary? If it does not increase annually at or above the rate of inflation, then you are actually earning less this year than last.

The U.S. Bureau of Labor Statistics announces annually what it costs for a family of four to live at an intermediate standard of living. The figure varies from area to area across the country. Current figures for your area can be determined by referring to the government publications available in most public and university libraries.

Using this Bureau figure as a convenient reference point, try to determine fair pay for the clergy of your church. First develop a cash compensation range which would run from 20 percent below mid-point to 20 percent above mid-point. (Remember that cash compensation includes salary and housing allowance but not benefits and business expenses.)

Within this plus-twenty/minus-twenty range, the minister's actual compensation would be determined by several factors: years of experience, amount of training, quality of service and demonstrated performance, job complexity, and the needs of the clergy family at its particular stage of the life cycle. Training should include continuing education. Job complexity entails size of congregation and number of staff persons supervised. You will need to refine these variables and attach specific dollar amounts to them in order to develop a scale for your situation. The mid-point figure would be that which is considered fair for a minister with a three-year seminary degree, about a dozen years of experience, and average abilities, serving a congregation of about 300 members. The work sheets in appendixes F and G will be useful as a starting point to help you develop a formula for your congregation.*

Clergy Taxes

Ministers need to be familiar with the special tax considerations that uniquely concern clergy. Space does not permit me to examine all of them here in depth. I strongly recommend that you find a qualified person with whom to consult, one who is familiar with the tax situation of the clergy, or else do your own research.* Either way, keep your information current, as the laws on these matters change from time to time.

The main thing to remember is to have your congregation distinguish clearly in its budget between compensation, benefits, and profession-related expenses such as travel. Further distinction within the compensation category needs to be made between salary and housing allowance.

Rental Allowance

Section 107 of the Internal Revenue Code provides that gross income for the minister does not include rental value of the parsonage or an allowance for housing. This item, called an exclusion, need not be reported as income. (It is included, however, in the calculation of your Social Security self-employment tax.) This exclusion from gross income must be an officially designated amount that is designated by the congregation or official body prior to its actual payment and use. The designation cannot be made retroactively at the end of the tax year. Treasury Regulation 1.107, which administers the Internal Revenue Code on this matter, defines "minister" and "home" ("a dwelling place") and what the housing allowance can be used for—such things as rent or purchase of housing and the expenses directly related to providing a home. These costs include mortgage payments, rent payments, utilities, maintenance, improvements, property taxes, insurance, furniture, landscaping, gardening, and furnishings.

There is no limitation in the code on the amount that can be designated for housing. However, revenue rulings in cases where the law has been applied by the courts have generally allowed an amount equal to the fair rental value of the home plus the cost of utilities, furnishings, and maintenance. The best course of action here is to be reasonable in the amount designated, even though there is no legal mandate setting a particular percentage of salary to be used for housing. Retired ministers are also eligible to exclude a portion of income actually used for housing.

When you are buying a home, property taxes and the interest portion of your mortgage payment are "deductible" if you itemize deductions. This deduction is in addition to the housing allowance "exclusion." Thus, you are legally entitled to a double savings on interest and property taxes—a generous tax break. Be sure, therefore, that your housing allowance is large enough. If you estimate too high, it is easy to include the unused excess as part of your income. Remember also that even if you are living in a church-owned home, you can still have a designated housing allowance to cover the items you pay for out of your own pocket, such items as lawn care, furnishings, maintenance, or utilities.

Professional Expenses

In addition to the housing allowance, tax savings can be realized by ministers for their professional expenses. The greatest expense of this sort is usually transportation.

Car

As described above, a church-owned or church-leased automobile is in most instances the preferred arrangement. You would then turn in to the congregation monthly for reimbursement a record of all expenses related to the professional use of the car. Accurate records of such use, including expenses related to it, must be maintained. The Internal Revenue Service gives you the option of taking a standard mileage deduction or figuring actual expenses. Actual expenses are usually preferred in an inflationary period. You should figure the deduction both ways, however, to see which method is more favorable for you. The IRS requires a contemporaneous record of your mileage with date, miles driven, and purpose of the trip. You should keep a small notebook in your car for this purpose. Estimates of mileage or of the percentage of total miles driven for business purposes are no longer acceptable, and should you be audited by the IRS you could lose a valuable deduction if your records are inadequate. Any professional travel you do by means other than the car is also deductible. Keep detailed records of your expenses for all travel done on church-related business, continuing education events, and other professional matters.

Entertainment

The professional expense most often neglected by ministers is that for entertainment. The IRS allows you to deduct expenses incurred that are "ordinary and necessary in the production of income." It is usually expected that you entertain families, individuals, or church groups. Whether you entertain in your home or at a restaurant, the expense incurred is deductible. Adequate records are required, including dates, names of persons entertained, and the purpose of the occasion. The cost of taking a hot dish to a church potluck supper is rarely recorded as a tax deduction by the clergy family, but it is a legitimate professional expense. A guest book in your home is one good way of having an accurate list of persons and dates for home entertainment. If you entertain church guests at a nearby restaurant, keep a receipt whenever the amount exceeds $25.00.

Gifts

Gifts to anyone with whom you have a ministerial relationship are also deductible. How many baby shower gifts have you given this year? How many books to couples you marry? The key to all these deductions is the discipline of writing down all such expenses. It could be well worth your time to adopt the habit. It takes only a minute or two now and then, but it will add up to a substantial tax savings at the end of the year.

Reducing Taxes

There are ways to delay taxes on some income until a later time when your tax bracket drops. Most clergy with modest incomes may think that tax shelters are complex or only for the wealthy. Actually, there are safe and sensible shelters by which you can ease your tax load. If your employer provides a pension program as one fringe benefit, you already enjoy one of the best tax shelters. You do not pay taxes on the money invested in a pension fund until you retire, at which time you will probably be in a more favorable tax situation. Some programs allow you to add to a pension plan in a lump sum, or to have a specified amount withheld regularly and put directly into this fund. Such amounts are not subject to tax until retirement.

There are a number of "do-it-yourself" retirement plans wherein persons can earmark some percentage of their earnings, up to a certain maximum, for retirement. Self-employed persons may qualify for a Keogh plan in which 15 percent of their income, up to a total of $7,500 a year, can be invested. In all of these plans, taxes on the amount invested are postponed until retirement. Persons who do not have a pension program should look into one of these options, not only for immediate tax savings but also as preparation for retirement.

When you sell a home, tax on the profit from the sale is postponed if you reinvest in another home of equal or greater value within the IRS deadline for replacement. You can escape taxes on up to $125,000 of that profit altogether if you are at least fifty-five years old and have lived in the home for three of the last five years prior to selling it. This benefit allows a person to "buy down" at the empty-nest phase of the life cycle, or to consider renting as an option, without owing a large sum of taxes on the sale of a home.

There are also ways to avoid taxes by creating custodian accounts or trust funds. One such plan enables you to accumulate money for sending a child to college and put it into such a fund. The assets actually belong to the child, whose tax bracket is naturally lower or nonexistent. The IRS thus gets less of your investment income. The same can be done for an elderly parent whom you may be helping to support. Some arrangements allow you to put property or stocks into a trust fund from which a child or elderly parent will receive the interest (thus saving you taxes on the interest income), while the property or stock will revert to you at the end of a stipulated period. It would be wise to seek out expert financial counsel if you see value in any of these plans.

Clergy Housing

The church-owned parsonage you live in may well have doubled in value in the last five years. Is that increased equity now in your pocket? Of course not! Church-owned housing was never intended by churches as a means to make money, either for the institution or for the minister. If fact, it has always been considered as only part of your total remuneration. Traditional plans to provide a home for the minister's family grew out of a more agrarian period of history when alternative housing was not really available in most communities, when the general economic picture was such that ministers were often paid in goods and services rather than in cash, and when renting was far more prevalent than it is today.

Even though times have changed greatly, the parsonage system has been retained in some denominations, largely for the purpose of administrative efficiency: the system facilitates the moving of clergy from one church to another. Also, in rural and small-town settings, housing is still not as readily available as in urban and suburban settings. For these and other reasons, church-owned housing systems will probably not soon disappear.

What appears to be taking place today, however, is a slow movement on the part of the congregations and denominations toward greater flexibility where housing is concerned. Clergy families clearly prefer the option of renting or buying their own housing. There is a clear correlation between housing and family morale.* Housing arrangements also affect the relationship between the clergy family and the congregation. Though some clergy families still prefer to live in church-owned housing, an increasing number feel that parsonages are "inhuman to family life," "an economic disaster," and "a put-down to the professional minister"; they impose "pressure on the famliy" and "a limitation on community witness." Most clergy families want the freedom to express themselves through the choice of home style, location, decoration, and furnishings. They want to assume responsibility for maintenance and taxes so that they will know what this experience is like for their parishioners. From an economic standpoint, these clergy families also want the opportunity to build equity as a hedge against inflation and as a preparation for retirement.

In certain localities a church-owned home may continue to be the best choice, even the preference of clergy who for one reason or another simply do not want to be involved with property ownership. However, any minister who looks seriously at the total scope of financial planning cannot avoid considering the option of home ownership, with all the hassles and benefits that go with it. Whatever choice you make, the question of home ownership requires a major decision. If you should decide to buy, you need to consider location, schools, and other factors in addition to the age and condition of the building itself.

Inflation may make the possibility of home ownership remote for the average minister. However, this same economic fact of life has greatly increased the value of church-owned housing and could be the vehicle for assisting clergy to make the transition. If the minister wants to buy the parsonage, an arrangement could probably be worked out which would cost the church little more than it is currently paying for housing.* Or the parsonage could be rented or sold, thereby creating funds for an adequate housing allowance. A little imagination, goodwill, sense of fair play, and some creative planning by the minister and congregation (assisted by sound guidance from financial experts in the community) could give birth to such viable possibilities.

Getting Ready for Retirement

One can never begin too early to think about retirement. It may be an unpleasant thought for some, especially if there are a lot of unresolved questions about that phase of the life cycle. But what are the important issues? Health is certainly one. How will you be feeling by age sixty-five or seventy? Activity is another. What will you do after retirement? Are you looking forward to limiting activity, or are you concerned about getting bored? A place to live is a major concern for many. Where would you like to live? What part of the country? In what type of housing? And of course, finances are probably the major concern for many. How much will you have to live on? Will it be enough? All of these are important questions for you to consider and, if married, to discuss with your partner. As you develop answers to these questions, you will be on your way to a plan for the retirement years.

Moreover, all of these issues require that you begin doing something now, whatever your age, if retirement is eventually to be what you would like it to be. For example, you must begin thinking about health long before age sixty-five. Start now, whatever your age, by forming good disciplines in such matters as nutrition, exercise, and time for contemplation, fun, and relaxation. Such habits prepare you for moving into retirement with a capacity to enjoy it.

Likewise, you should not wait until retirement to begin working on your primary relationship. If work and children have enabled you to ignore marital tension over the years, you may be dreading the retirement years when you and your spouse will be together more as a couple. For those who have been totally absorbed in children or work, and have to adjust to each other all over again, the empty-nest and retirement periods can be difficult. A long-neglected marriage can become the central fact of life. For better or worse, marital conflict may surface and need to be faced. Begin now to work on this important part of your life. It can be almost like starting fresh. Indeed, retirement can mean almost a new marriage. This radical transition can be made much easier if you begin now to get reacquainted and to deepen the communication between you.

The financial arena is also one in which advance planning can make possible a smoother transition into retirement and help you realize some of your dreams for the later years. How much money will you need to live in a comfortable style? How much will Social Security provide? What can you expect from your pension program? From savings and investments? Will you continue to earn some money? For how long? What about housing? Will you continue to reside in your present home or will you want something smaller? If you live in a parsonage, what plans are you making for retirement housing?

If your denomination insists on church-owned housing, perhaps you could help initiate consideration of a housing equity plan that, like the pension program, would be controlled and managed by the denomination. Required contributions by the congregation could go into a central fund as part of your fringe benefit package. Such a plan could guarantee at least some equity at retirement. For example, a conservative 6 percent annual return on a small contribution amounting to 4 percent of an annual $12,000 cash salary (a modest $40 a month) would build to $6,577 in ten years, $18,508 in twenty years, and $37,017 in forty years. That amount is not anywhere near the equity you would have realized in owning a home over the same period, but it is much more than most retiring clergy have accumulated; it would help immensely toward providing you with retirement housing.

Some clergy couples plan to move into a retirement community. A few denominations provide retirement housing for religious professionals. Harry and Joanne, a retired clergy couple I know, have made such a transition. Joanne was not employed outside the home until six years before Harry's retirement. Her part-time job at a local school took the financial pressure off. The extra income enabled them to save for retirement, bought them a health insurance plan, and enabled them to be more generous to some of their favorite causes. They never owned a home, having lived in parsonages or rented homes throughout their married life. They had a feeling of "being taken care of" by the respective congregations they served. Joanne told us that "people take more interest in you when you live in a parsonage." Upon retirement, Harry and Joanne moved into a community for retired religious professionals. Harry's parents had spent their retirement years in the same community, and Harry and Joanne had for several years made annual visits to this community, for the purpose of getting acquainted with the people there prior to their own moving in.

Today they feel safe and secure in this familiar environment. "If anything goes wrong, they'll take care of us here," Harry explained. This couple feels that theirs is an ideal retirement setting. They claim to be "on easy street" now. Formerly their priorities had been educating their children and keeping the family well. Now they enjoy traveling to see the kids.

Harry and Joanne are just one illustration of successful retirement. There is an advantage in planning ahead, and starting early. There are many excellent resources available to assist you in your planning. A few of these are listed in the annotated bibliography.

5. Additional Resources for Clergy and Laity

Savings and Investments

The last few years have witnessed a large growth in the number of financial institutions and the services they offer. Today there are more options available to us than ever before for saving and investing. It is important in financial planning to know something about these many options and how to evaluate them in the context of an inflationary economy.

Most of us are familiar with the corner bank. We have used many of its services: checking accounts, savings accounts, safe-deposit boxes, personal loans, perhaps a mortgage loan, credit card services, the purchase of traveler's checks, maybe a notary public. Many of us have a checking account at a bank and a savings account at a savings-and-loan institution, which for years was allowed by law to offer a slightly higher rate of interest than the bank. In addition to passbook savings accounts, savings-and-loan institutions also offer various longer-term certificates of deposit, which earn higher interest but tie up your funds for a specified period. Six-month Treasury bills have recently become fairly popular, paying very competitive interest for a relatively short investment period. They do, however, require a relatively large minimum investment. If you have a savings reserve and can afford to be without a sizable sum for six months or longer, it may make good sense to exercise this savings option.

Ongoing changes in the laws that regulate financial institutions, and in such institutions themselves as well as in other business enterprises seeking part of the financial action, make it necessary to stay abreast of the latest developments if in your savings program you would stay abreast of inflation. Inflation, coupled with the regulations that set ceilings of various sorts on the interest rates payable by banks and by savings-and-loan associations, has called into question the conventional wisdom of Ben Franklin. It no longer "pays to save" if your savings earn at rates below the level of inflation.

You receive two returns from any investment: (1) interest after taxes and (2) a gain or loss from the change in the purchasing power of your investment. You must calculate both returns to know the full earnings of your investment choice. The same is true, of course, with respect to borrowing money in today's economy. Though I am hesitant to set forth a general maxim in this regard, it is nevertheless conceivable that you could be better off today to borrow than to save. This does not mean that you should increase your indebtedness and forget savings. It does mean that you need to be much wiser today in your choice of savings options, since many of them could turn out to be losing options.

The credit union is another important financial institution. Credit unions are nonprofit volunteer institutions, carefully regulated by law. As a member you buy shares (invest savings), for which you receive a return (interest). With their low overhead, credit unions can offer loans and other services at very competitive rates. Some offer share drafts that are similar to checking accounts which earn interest.

Thrift associations and finance companies are also available in most areas. Since they take greater risks in loaning money, they usually require substantially higher rates of interest on their loans. I usually recommend that individuals and families not borrow from such a resource, as its exorbitant interest rates may tend to perpetuate their financial difficulties.

There are numerous investment opportunities available today beyond those of the well-known financial establishments: stocks, bonds, mutual funds, certain types of insurance, including annuities, and money market funds. In a time of high interest rates the money market funds have much to offer, including interest that fluctuates with the market. Most of them require minimum deposits but are flexible in allowing withdrawals without penalties.

Real estate is an attractive investment choice in certain areas. Partnership investment opportunities are available, where the small investor, with a group of partners, can purchase income-producing property such as an apartment or duplex. The investors who put these partnerships together may offer to manage the property for a small percentage of the profit, so that all you have to do is put up some cash and then sit back and watch it grow. Real estate is sometimes the best hedge against inflation, as homeowners well know. Since economic conditions vary so much from place to place, and the economy generally is in constant flux, I recommend that you seek expert local consultation before making any investments. You need to know personally some of the financial resource persons in your community so you can make responsible referrals of parishioners with whom you are counseling. These financial experts are also valuable persons to bring in for any educational experiences you may hope to offer in the congregation.

Credit

Laura and Frank came to our pastoral counseling center on referral from their pastor. They had been married for twelve years and had two children, a ten-year-old son and a six-year-old daughter. Laura phoned for the appointment. She complained of having been embarrassed by her husband in front of some church friends. She had been so angry that she took the children and went to her mother's home for a few days. The staff counselor encouraged her to come in and bring her husband in too.

In further conversation Laura expressed her wish that Frank would spend more time with her, listen to her, and really share instead of talking from behind the newspaper or with one eye on the television. Frank complained that Laura was a sloppy housekeeper and was running up more and more debts on their credit cards. As the session continued, it became clear that Laura, by foot-dragging in her role as homemaker, and by extravagant spending, was simply expressing her frustration and anger at Frank over their lack of communication. After some initial blaming and counter-blaming, Laura and Frank began to communicate more directly about their frustrations, their feelings of inadequacy in their roles, and eventually their hopes for their relationship.

A large proportion of credit abuse and extravagant spending fits a pattern similar to that of Frank and Laura. The unwise use of credit is often a symptom of a larger marital problem; it may even be a misdirected effort to cope with the strain in the relationship. Not all credit abuse stems from this source, of course. Families are bombarded with credit options today. Contemporary Americans live in a credit-oriented society. Most financial institutions, except for credit unions, charge penalties for early payoff of loans, thus encouraging people to prolong their indebtedness. Credit is too easily obtained. You have probably received unsolicited credit cards yourself through the mail. In addition to easy credit, the heavy bombardment of advertising through the media creates a climate of wanting all sorts of goods and services—and immediate gratification. Today's families are "sitting ducks" for credit abuse.

An attorney who is a specialist in family law and works with couples in the process of dissolving their marriage reports that many clients in his affluent Claremont, California, community are surprised to learn that they have far fewer assets to divide than they assumed. Mostly they have debts! Even though these families have high incomes, it is not uncommon for them to be making high monthly mortgage payments and car payments; their furniture is largely owned by the bank or finance company, and monthly payments on store and bank credit cards are all near the maximum allowed. It is precisely these middle-income people who are often most vulnerable to credit abuse and who most frequently visit the financial counseling agencies. Income has doubled in a decade, and that leaves many persons with an exaggerated impression of their affluence. Most people also lack the management skills necessary to cope with an inflationary and changing economy.

Credit, like cash, is a medium of exchange. It allows us to obtain goods and services now in exchange for a promise to pay in the future. What is involved is a contract for the use of future income. It is based on trust that you will be both able and willing to pay when the bill comes due. There are several kinds of credit arrangements: (1) Regular charge accounts permit you to buy items or services when you need them; if you pay the bill within a given period of time there is no charge for the use of the money. (2) Revolving charge accounts allow you to charge up to some limit and pay a stipulated part monthly; as long as you have a balance due at the end of the monthly billing period you will be charged interest. (3) Installment or time-payment plans permit you to buy high-cost items like furniture or a car; you make a down payment and pay off the balance, including the finance charges, over a period of months or years. (4) Loans of various kinds are also available with varying terms from banks and credit unions.

With all these forms of credit available, some big questions arise: How much is it costing you to use this money? Will the item you purchase last as long as it takes you to pay for it? It is discouraging to be paying for a car or a piece of furniture long after it is worn out.

You should learn to shop for credit. Charges vary. If you get confused by the percentages quoted, ask for the dollar amounts. Before you accept the credit offered by a car dealer, check with your bank or credit union to see if you can borrow the same money for less. Many people shop wisely for a new car and then throw their savings away carelessly on expensive credit arrangements. You should know that revolving charge accounts at the store can range from 12 percent to 18 percent, while small loan companies often charge from 30 percent to 40 percent.

In an inflationary economy, however, it is no longer the case that you are always better off to save ahead and pay cash. You have to be very careful in choosing a savings plan or you may actually be losing money while your cash sits in the bank. Remember, too, that the item you wish to purchase may well cost more six months or a year from now. Indeed, it is likely that the inflation-induced price boost during those months will more than offset the interest earned on your savings over the same period of time; it may even more than offset the interest you would have to pay if you were to borrow now and make the purchase right away. So at times it definitely pays to borrow rather than save. This can be especially true of durable items such as cars, houses, and furniture.

Credit, therefore, can work for you. It can allow you to take advantage of sales and avoid price increases. Combined with a wise savings plan, it can help you even more. If you save at a favorable rate (such as is possible in a money market fund or with Treasury bills) and then use credit for which you have shopped judiciously, you can come out ahead. In an inflationary period it is possible, by saving and borrowing at the same time, to maximize your use of resources. You can perhaps receive more money in interest on your savings than you spend for using bank or credit-union money.

The wise use of a bank credit card is a good example of this. Instead of taking money out of savings to purchase an item, you may choose in an inflationary period to leave your money in the bank, earning interest, while you charge the item on your bank card, thereby using the bank's money for thirty days or so absolutely free of charge. If you pay for the item in full at the billing date, you avoid any interest charge on the credit cards. You simply use them for convenience in shopping and take advantage of having free use of the bank's money for thirty days or until billing takes place. Always pay off the full balance each month on all these cards so as to avoid all interest charges.

This practice of paying all balances monthly also acts as a deterrent against charging more items than you can afford. It is a good rule of thumb not to have more credit than you could pay off in sixty days at most without disrupting your budget. It is also a good rule to borrow only for budgeted items. That is, use credit as part of your spending plan, not outside of it.

If you do use credit and pay interest, remember that the interest is a deductible item at tax time. Keep a record of interest paid, especially on large items. It is wise also to hold to a minimum the number of credit cards you use at any given time. Most revolving accounts charge 18 percent on the first $500 and 12 percent after that. If you charge $500 on each of two different cards, you would pay 18 percent on the amount charged on each—18 percent of $1,000—whereas if you charged the entire $1,000 on one account, you would pay 18 percent on the first $500 and only 12 percent on the second $500.

Most important of all, do not expand your credit as your income increases. It is likely that inflation will have more than consumed the increase, and that you are no more affluent, probably even less affluent than before, in terms of real purchasing power.

Life Insurance

Most of us will survive the perils of birth, childhood, and early and middle adulthood, and live long enough to reach retirement years. However, the risk of death by illness or accident exists, and its financial impact on dependent survivors can be disastrous. If covered by Social Security, you will have some assistance, especially while children are living with the surviving spouse; but there are gaps in this coverage, and at any period of the life cycle Social Security is at best only a minimal help.

Life insurance is a crucial part of any financial plan. If a breadwinner dies, the insurance will pay for funeral expenses and settlement of the estate, provide money for the family while it is adjusting to new conditions, and assure some stability in family income while the children are growing up.

The insurance needs of a family change with circumstances and through each phase of the life cycle. In a family where there are children and the breadwinning rests largely with one spouse, it would be foolish and risky not to cover that spouse with as much protection as possible. As children leave the nest the need for insurance is reduced. If both spouses are employed, the risk is smaller yet. At such a point in the life cycle of the family, insurance may be viewed less as protection of income for the immediate future and more in terms of long-range planning for retirement.

Different kinds of insurance exist to fulfill these different needs. From a functional viewpoint there are really three kinds of life insurance: term, whole life, and endowment. Everything else is a modification or combination of one or more of these.

Term insurance provides protection only. It is the least expensive form of life insurance because no cash benefits—no savings—accrue. In the early years of marriage and while there are young children, it is important to have the maximum amount of protection. Since you can probably afford much more term insurance than whole life, I strongly recommend that you use this form of insurance at this phase of the family life cycle. It provides the most protection for the least money.

Whole life, sometimes called ordinary life or straight life, provides protection plus a savings component. Whereas term insurance increases in cost as you get older, whole life is based on a level premium. Whole life insurance is more costly than term insurance, especially during the early years. The forced savings aspect is often viewed as a benefit to those persons who lack the discipline required to save money on a regular basis. However, the interest rate on the savings dimension of whole life is very modest. You can do much better by buying term insurance and investing in alternative savings instruments that yield greater per-dollar benefits. Since investing always involves some element of risk, however, there are no guarantees that this plan (term plus invested savings) will do better than the whole life plan (protection plus cash benefits). The major reason for going with term insurance is that you will be able to provide considerably more protection for a smaller monthly premium, and that is important for younger families on a limited budget. Remember, the main purpose of insurance is protection, not savings.

Endowment plans are basically savings plans with a term feature.

Premiums are higher for this form of insurance than for term or whole life; they are paid for a specified period of years, after which time the returns come back to the insured. Some endowment plans bring tax benefits, but generally they bring you less interest than you could get by putting your money into savings at your bank. Like whole life, however, endowment plans have that disciplined savings feature. They actually enable you to accumulate a given sum by a given age and hence can be a valuable element in planning for retirement. They also have the insurance feature, so that if you die prior to retirement, the benefits can go in full to your beneficiary. In an inflationary period the savings feature of all insurance plans should be carefully evaluated, since their interest rates are lower than those of other investment options.

There are a variety of group insurance options also, some of which may be available to you or provided as fringe benefits. Generally these group programs are term insurance. Since the group term insurance which I currently receive as a fringe benefit is approximately equal to the unpaid mortgage on our home, it serves the function of mortgage insurance, guaranteeing that if I should die, my family would have a debt-free home.

Whatever insurance package you put together should be calculated (along with Social Security benefits) to get your children through school and out of the nest. So-called reducing term insurance is one good option, because for each year that you survive, the amount of insurance needed decreases. Be sure to keep abreast of inflation by recalculating your insurance requirements on a regular basis.

Some people use insurance for building their estate or for retirement planning. Others opt to use it strictly for protection. In an inflationary period, with budgets tightening, you should evaluate carefully your insurance program. The industry is always trying to sell you more, but you should buy only what meets your real needs and fits your overall financial plan.

Also, do not hesitate to shop around, as prices will vary. Consumer magazines and organizations often publish helpful guidelines for people shopping to meet their insurance needs. As you look for life insurance remember that you want a policy which is noncancellable and guaranteed renewable, provides for a guaranteed premium, has worldwide coverage, and relates you to an agent who is trustworthy.

Insurance protection in relation to your home, automobile, health, and potential disability should be considered carefully. Be sure that your church provides disability insurance. Also, be sure you know what is covered by the homeowner's policy if you live in church-owned housing. Your personal belongings, including your library, may not be covered, and you may need a tenant policy similar to that of a renter to protect against loss of your property. If you own your own home, an annual review of your homeowner's insurance should confirm that current replacement costs will be covered. Both disability insurance and home protection should be considered fringe benefits by the church, along with the costs of auto insurance for your business use of the car, a health plan, and also some amount of group term life insurance. Many clergy today, especially those engaged in counseling, are also considering malpractice insurance. If your congregation is not currently considering all of these items in its fringe benefits package, you have some negotiating to do.

Consumer Guidelines

A few years ago there was truth in the old saying, "You get what you pay for." In the long run it paid to buy quality name brands rather than trying to save money through the purchase of less expensive, "off-brand" products—which usually turned out to be inferior in one way or another. This is no longer always true. There is still great variation in product quality, but there are substantial price differences among many products of the same quality. In fact, the very same product can vary in price by as much as 30 to 40 percent. This makes shopping much more complex, as there is an extraordinary scope for gain or loss in such a market. Shopping is not quite at the point of the old "bargain and dicker" system found in many parts of the world, where you are expected to quibble over price, but it is getting closer to that on some items.

As a result of this changing reality it is wise to shop carefully, especially for the more costly items. You might also consider buying in the off-season or at the end of the season. There are enormous payoffs today for those who take time to do effective shopping, and enormous losses for those who do not.

In the food marketplace, it is wise to avoid stores that use stamps and games; benefits of that kind are paid for by increased prices. Coupon shopping and mailing in forms for cash refunds can be a means to substantial savings. Working at this in even a casual manner can knock 10 to 15 percent off your monthly bill. Buying generic names and local store brands of many food products, rather than the nationally advertised brands, can save you additional dollars. It may pay you to write out your list of needed items before you go shopping, as this tends to prevent impulse buying while you are in the store. You will probably save plenty if you can stick to what is on your list.

There are advantages and disadvantages to taking the children with you to the grocery store. On the positive side, the experience will probably impart to them some appreciation of the cost of things they otherwise take for granted. At the same time, however, children tend to pressure you to buy whatever strikes their fancy, or what they saw advertised on television, and you may end up spending more.

If you are one whose shopping is prompted more by your stomach than your head, be sure to shop on a full stomach, not when you are hungry. Stock up when items are on sale. Larger quantities are usually cheaper. If you have a freezer, you might make an occasional trip to a "day-old" bakery and save considerably.

There are many ways to cut costs in services as well. You might consider doing your own maintenance on the house or the car—at least some of the minor chores like yard work or changing engine oil. With skyrocketing energy costs, you could even leave the car at home and walk or ride a bike. Turning the thermostat down a degree or two on water heater and furnace, and up a few degrees on the air conditioner, will effect significant savings with little or no long-range cost in personal discomfort. Most of us have become such slaves to convenience that we may feel deprived at first, as we begin to change our style of living and consuming, but it can be done. It can even be fun—well, at least a challenge!

Preparing a Will

Included among the family service resources in most communities are representatives of the legal profession. Attorneys play an important role as consultants on various legal aspects of financial planning. Preparing a will is one important example of this kind of assistance.

Too many persons postpone making wills. There are several important reasons why drawing up a will deserves high priority.

If you should die without a will, you have given up your right to decide how your estate will be divided. It makes no sense to strive for good stewardship throughout your lifetime and then at the end let the state make all the legal decisions. Preparing a will can save time and money in taxes and legal expenses for your survivors. The $100 or so it may cost is money well spent!

A will enables you to name an executor who can manage your estate according to your instructions. You can also choose the guardian for any of your dependent children. You can create trusts so that the persons and/or organizations you specify will receive the benefits. You can leave an anatomic gift such as an eye or kidney for whomever may need it in your community, and you can spell out in detail any instructions you may have concerning your funeral.

Before you visit a lawyer, talk about these issues with your loved ones and make some notes in preparation for the legal consultation. Have current legal names and addresses for all persons named in your will. Also, write out the details of your financial situation, including all property, insurance, and pension information. If you have been divorced, you should bring along any existing settlement agreements.

Once you have a will it should be kept in a safe place, perhaps a safe-deposit box, and periodically reviewed to determine if it expresses your current wishes. It can be updated by an attorney whenever your situation changes.

A will is your last gift to your loved ones. It can reflect your values and show your love and concern. It can underscore your commitments and express your gratitude to God and the church—and any other special causes you deem worthy—as well as to your family. Give the matter of a will your careful thought, and do something about it soon. Don't put it off!

Your search for a suitable attorney to draw up your own will can be an excellent avenue for discovering a valuable resource person who may assist you in other ways. In fact, the more resource persons you come to know personally in your community, the better prepared you are to counsel others in financial crises, to refer people needing specialized help, and to design and staff your church's educational program for families and individuals.

6. Educational Programs on Financial Planning

We have spoken of the financial issues faced by individuals and families at crucial transition points in their life cycle. Marriage, the birth of a child, children leaving home, retirement—these are not only times of celebration and grief; they are also events requiring fiscal adjustments. Every phase of the life cycle involves a letting go of the past and an embracing of new possibilities for the future. Financial planning can smooth the transition through each such period of change. Life-cycle transitions are pregnant with growth opportunities, and religious institutions are in a strategic position to help persons realize the positive potential of each period of life.

Programming Throughout the Life Cycle

Joe and Sally found that much of their church's educational program is built around the life-cycle transitions.

Included in the program at First Church is a workshop design for those "about to be married" and another for the "recently married." Workshops are offered approximately every three months. There are a variety of important components in the premarital design, including a presentation by a medical doctor, an experience in building communication skills led by a marriage counselor, a presentation by the pastor on the religious and theological dimensions of marriage, and a financial-planning session that involves a panel of community resource persons. Leadership for these workshops comes mostly from the church's own membership. Meetings are held in the educational wing on Sunday afternoon and evening. The workshop is supplemented by two or three counseling sessions with the minister who is to officiate at the wedding. A parish that does not have a sufficient number of couples for such a workshop could try to develop an ecumenical model in cooperation with nearby churches.

First Church is sensitive to the fact that many persons entering marriage today bring with them children from a previous marriage. To help these families with what can be a difficult transition, the church periodically conducts a workshop specifically for them. The focus for this group is heavily weighted toward psychological components such as grief work (focusing on the divorce or death which ended the earlier marriage) and family communication skills. Family financial planning is included in the design for this workshop because money is often a sticky dimension for second-marriage families. Sometimes old battles are carried forward with respect to children, especially as regards child-care payments, alimony, and travel between the two sets of parents. These families need help in resolving the issues inherited from former relationships as well as in contracting with respect to new ones. Such family systems are very complex. The church's effort to address the issues involved meets a real need.

An adult singles group meets in First Church on a regular basis. A modified form of the workshop for remarrieds is held occasionally for the recently divorced members of this singles group. Here the workshop focus is on grief and dissolution issues as well as on communication skills and money issues facing single persons.

Younger couples are encouraged to participate in the church's marriage enrichment programs, which include a focus on communications, values and rules, and family financial planning. For Joe and Sally, the first training in family financial planning came in such an enrichment seminar.

The church also holds intergenerational workshops for families with adolescents. These workshops focus on the important transition period of adolescence, when communication can be a problem. Here parents and teens talk about changes in values and in family roles and rules as well as the changing relationship of adolescents and parents. Since so much communication between parents and teens is about money, family financial planning is an important ingredient of these workshops too.

First Church also offers a preretirement workshop for people in their later mid-years. Here the focus is on helping persons to cope with change and loss related to the empty nest, and to anticipate their retirement years. Financial planning is again an important part of the workshop design.

Recently the church has added a new program for widows and widowers, in which there is strong emphasis on resolving grief constructively. Other issues relevant for this phase of the life cycle are also considered: financial planning, housing, nutrition, transportation, the need for a support group, and health matters.

Workshops for Women

In addition to a life-cycle focus, there is a need to design events around certain other homogeneous groupings, for example, single women. At the Smoky Mountain Center for Independent Studies in Lake Junaluska, North Carolina, a pilot workshop design for women was recently prepared under a grant from the Interfaith Council for Family Financial Planning. Participants in the workshop included women who had never married as well as those who had undergone divorce or experienced a husband's death.

This pilot design focused on the adult life cycle, attitudes toward money, and community resources for financial planning. It brought in representatives from banking, insurance, Social Security, and law. Participants actually worked on a financial plan and made some commitments to first steps. They experienced support from one another and gained valuable information and skills for helping themselves in the financial arena. The formerly married agreed that if they had had greater familiarity with planning, they would have been better prepared to cope with singleness today.

The Financial Aid Director at the School of Theology at Claremont, who attended this pilot workshop for women, has since offered similar programs for women on campus. Her workshops have been well attended. She used as consultants women from the local community—a feature that is additionally appreciated because it provides valuable role models for women preparing themselves for professional positions in the community. Churches as well as seminaries should hold workshops for single women.

Many women, single and married alike, have been seriously limited in the area of financial planning and management skills by the sexist attitudes in a society that associates money with power and power with masculine prerogatives. These attitudes are implicit in Social Security regulations, banking and credit practices, and unequal remuneration for women in most employment. Many women have been in marriages where their husbands have not only earned but also managed the money. When such women become single they need experience as well as skills in order to begin to take care of themselves responsibly in the financial arena.

Workshops for Clergy

There are several opportune times in the professional life cycle of clergy for financial-planning education. The seminary years are a good beginning point. A few schools are now offering credit courses, and others offer noncredit workshops. At the School of Theology at Claremont a workshop is offered annually for graduating seniors and their spouses.

Five to ten years into the ministry is another good time for assessment and further refinement of financial planning by clergy, as is mid-career, about fifteen to twenty years into the ministry. The preretirement period is yet another opportune time for offering financial-planning education to groups of ministers.

Participation in a financial-planning workshop provides clergy with a cluster of competencies: (1) the ability to analyze personal and family goals and priorities; (2) the ability to assess a variety of financial resources pertinent to these goals throughout the life span; (3) the skill to design a comprehensive personal and family financial plan, reflecting goals, priorities, and resources; (4) the ability to use such a plan as a means of expressing values, attaining goals, and fulfilling priorities; (5) the skill to evaluate and modify plans to meet changing social, economic, and life-cycle conditions, and (6) the means of functioning more effectively in obtaining the financial resources on which the plan is structured.

This broad survey of financial-planning models for stages across the life cycle, as well as for homogeneous groups such as women or clergy, is offered in the hope that you will discover a place where you can begin. Not every congregation has the resources of First Church, but you can select one or more areas appropriate to your particular situation. A small congregation might plan an intergenerational event. Perhaps you could begin by encouraging your denomination to plan a training event for ministers. The Interfaith Council for Family Financial Planning has resources to help you get started.*

Designing Educational Events for Laity

After you have participated in a financial-planning workshop, you may be ready to help design such an event for lay persons in your parish or community. Designing educational events for others will of course increase your own competency in financial planning.

My first involvement in financial-planning education occurred when I was teaching a seminary summer course on family counseling and wanted to include a study unit on problems related to money. I brought to the class several community resource persons in the areas of banking, insurance, law, and theology. In subse-quent designs I included additional resource persons, and eventually I began to discover a group of persons in the community who were good communicators, worked well as a team of experts, and understood what I was attempting to accomplish in the course.

Church education committees too can learn as they get involved in developing an educational program in family financial planning. First Church did not start out with a whole range of workshops. At first, small components were added to existing classes for adults, couples, singles, and youth groups. The premarital workshop was the first major undertaking. Other workshops were added later.

One of the things First Church learned from its experience was that education programs are more effective when they are directed to a focus group that clearly has common interests and needs. Homogeneous groupings encourage open sharing and allow the leaders to prepare content relevant to all those involved.

The educational planning committee at First Church gradually became more skillful in identifying the needs and interests of various groups. They came to realize that learning is directly related to the satisfaction of the participants' needs, to their problems and anxieties, to the questions they are asking, to the kinds of information they lack, and to the skills that require sharpening. Appropriate resources and learning activities can then be matched to this profile of needs.

There are various ways to learn about the needs of the focus group. At First Church written questionnaires were used and several personal interviews were conducted to gather information. Oftentimes the pastor had a good picture of various individuals and families through his counseling, home visitation, and other personal contacts. Also, the planning committee for each educational event included persons from the target group.

With the needed background data in hand, committee members were ready to set some clear goals for the learning experience. What specific information did they want the group to have? What new attitudes did they want to expose them to? What new behavior did they want them to adopt? For example, at the conclusion of one family financial-planning event participants were to be able to: (1) describe the various family life-cycle stages and identify the characteristics and financial issues of each; (2) list their family's resources, including money, skills, experience, and education; (3) articulate clear ideas about protecting these resources—for example, through the appropriate use of insurance that would adequately satisfy family needs, and (4) begin to design a family financial plan, including values clarification and goal setting as well as a spending plan that would cover day-to-day operations, reserves, and long-range needs.

Goals, then, should deal with the needs and interests of the workshop participants and be related to the specific things they will be helped to know and do. Having clear goals will help you greatly later, when you begin to evaluate the effectiveness of your design. Churches are often unsure about the success of their efforts because they have not stated their goals clearly at the outset. Goals should be realistic and attainable within the scope of your design. If they are stated simply and clearly in your promotional materials, participants will know better just what to expect.

With a clear set of goals, the planning committee at First Church was ready to determine the content of the workshop. In planning an educational event for families, it was decided to give some attention to the following: (1) family dynamics and the way money is used in family communication; (2) the family life cycle: (3) family values clarification; (4) current financial issues—for example, recession and inflation and their effect on the family; (5) the ingredients of a family financial plan—identifying the basic concepts and planning skills; (6) family goals and the development of a financial plan to attain those goals, and (7) available community financial institutions and such topics as insurance, investments, housing, credit, and the legal aspects of financial planning.

Once they had decided on the content for their event the planning committee began to list the resources available to them. This list included community resources such as literature, audiovisuals, agencies such as banks, credit unions, law firms, and insurance companies, and human resources such as bankers, lawyers, insurance agents, real-estate experts, investment brokers, and religious professionals. (For some other sources see the bibliography.)

There are a variety of experts in most communities. The time limits and interests of your particular group, as well as the specific availability of persons in your area, will require that you make appropriate selections. If personal resources are limited, you may need to depend more on printed materials or media. For groups of clergy it would be appropriate to give some attention to the theology of money as well as to the application of financial-planning concepts to family counseling and educational program designing.

The committee at First Church was now ready to select the educational methods they would use. They wanted to involve the participants in the learning experience as fully as possible. There would necessarily be some presentations for the sharing of information, but these would be combined with activities directly involving the participants. The committee had learned, from earlier efforts in designing workshops, that content needed to be applied and assimilated along the way or it would not be used later. They decided to incorporate various approaches to experiential learning: (1) structured values-clarification exercises; (2) homework projects between sessions, including some family communication practice time; (3) small group sharing, and (4) a simulation game.

Experiential learning activities allow participants to become involved and more responsible for their own learning. In essence, these activities or exercises are practice opportunities. Too often educational designs include good information but little or no chance for a "hands on" experience. It is through group discussion and role play, and actually making plans and budgets, that persons begin to assimilate and personalize learning.

Design in hand, the planning committee at First Church was ready to recruit and train the leadership for their event. The church's professional staff were not experts in financial planning, but they had developed expertise in program designing and in bringing together a team of financial consultants.

It took time to build a team of experts in the area of family financial planning. Some members of the resource team were discovered in the congregation. Others were added from the community at large. Through experience it was learned that it was important to bring the team of experts together for a preworkshop planning session. As they talked together about the program objectives, they were helped to see how their contributions fit into the total design and they understood better the needs and interests of the focus group. The insurance expert, for example, saw that the presentation on insurance might be directed toward showing a family how to procure protection for its maximal benefit over the life cycle, rather than pushing whatever package was currently popular. The obvious risk is that a few professionals may see their participation as an opportunity to sell their products or services. They must be helped to understand that the objective is education in a broad sense, not sales.

Your community resource team can assist your church's planning committee in putting together the final structure of a workshop design. The ingredients will include the statement of goals, outline of content areas to be covered, the selected methods which will attempt to mix experiential learning with content presentations, the desired environment with a view of assuring comfort and sufficient space, and the necessary time limits. Once the structure for the event takes shape, the schedule is ready to be sent out along with publicity for recruiting participants.

At the conclusion of every workshop, First Church does an evaluation. If they have followed the steps carefully in designing their educational event, the criteria for evaluation are clear. Did they meet the objectives? The committee gets written feedback from all participants on what in the program was most useful and what was least helpful. From this feedback, committee members learn what is worth repeating and what may need to be added, dropped, or modified. The objective in evaluation is to learn from each experience in order to improve future workshops.

Evaluative feedback should cover not only the design of the workshop but also the leadership, content, and workshop setting. Feedback from the leadership team as well as the participants can be helpful. Anonymous written feedback is usually better than oral, since some persons will be more candid that way. Delayed feedback (a follow-up questionnaire after a month or two, for example) can show how workshop skills and learnings are still being applied in the weeks following. Whatever evaluation procedures you use should be planned in advance and viewed as part of the total design for the workshop.

Workshop designs will vary for different groups. Financial management needs vary for persons and families in different circumstances and at different phases of the life cycle. Topics and content will thus vary for each group even though all of the groups have some common financial tasks: to learn the major concepts of financial planning through the life cycle, to know about options for protecting their resources, to set goals in keeping with their values, to discover community resources, and to increase consumer proficiency.

The goal of education in family finance is to attempt to increase persons' self-esteem by giving them some handles which will help them both feel and be more in charge of their lives. A long-range family financial-planning program in your church will also open up ministry opportunities for a wide range of lay persons with varying expertise. In time, you can build an effective team of leaders to carry out a variety of educational endeavors. Remember, it takes time to develop successful programs, so start small and plan thoroughly.

The Challenge Facing the Church

There is no question but that the family is in great ferment today. Roles are changing. Patterns of family life are in flux. Values are up in the air, and effective family models are scarce. If money is one of the major problems facing families today, then religious institutions and religious leaders should be gearing up to help them deal more creatively with their financial concerns. The churches obviously do not have all the answers, but they can provide a place and a climate for creative exploration.

They can also help families bring together the best from their religious tradition, including biblical stewardship guidelines, and the best available expertise from the community for sound financial planning. Such a wholistic approach to planning is simply not available anywhere else. The church can meet an urgent need.

It is time to get our heads out of the sand and our hands out of our pockets! We live in a money world. There is no arena other than the church that has more potential, or greater challenge, for helping persons address the crucial value issues of our time.

Appendix A
Family Life Cycle

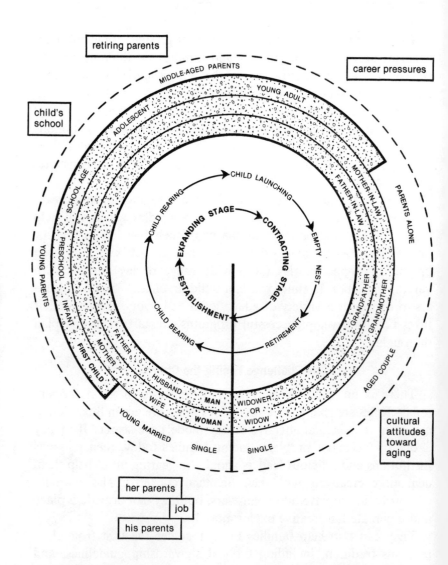

1) **Life-Cycle Changes**
   (two inner circles with arrows)

2) **Personal Identity**
   & Role Changes
   (three shaded circles)

3) **Family Structure Changes**
   (outer circle)

4) **Dominant Family**
   & Environmental Forces
   (boxes surrounding circle)

Appendix B

Monthly Expense Planning Sheet

Monthly Income:

1. Spouse	$_____
2. Spouse	_____
3. Other	_____
4. Other	_____
TOTAL	_____

Monthly Spending Plan:

1. Church and charities	_____
2. Rent or mortgage	_____
3. Utilities and telephone	_____
4. Maintenance and insurance	_____
5. Taxes	_____
6. Car: gas, maintenance, insurance	_____
7. Food: home and eating out	_____
8. Clothing: purchase and care	_____
9. Insurance: life and medical	_____
10. Education	_____
11. Subscriptions	_____
12. Recreation and amusements	_____
13. Doctor and dentist	_____
14. Medicine and drugs	_____
15. Savings for short-range reserves	_____
16. Savings for mid-range reserves	_____
17. Savings for future capital	_____
18. Other	_____
TOTAL	_____

From Appendix C (brace spanning items 15–17)

Reserves and Future Capital

	Jan	Feb	Mar	Apr	May	June	July	Aug	Sept	Oct	Nov	Dec
Reserves for Short-Range Goals												
1. Income taxes												
2. Property taxes												
3. Homeowner's insurance												
4. Home furnishings and furniture			(Amounts set aside each month in savings accounts or credit union shares or money market funds so that money will be available when semiannual or annual payments come due)									
5. Christmas												
6. Car insurance												
7. Life insurance (if paid annually)												
8. Vacation												
9. Maintenance												
10. Medical and dental												
11.												
12.												
Reserves for Mid-Range Goals												
13. Home improvement												
14. Next car			(Amounts set aside each month so that money will be available when the time comes for these outlays to be made)									
15. Special trip												
16. Major appliances												
17.												
18.												
Future Capital for Long-Range Goals												
19. College education												
20. Down payment on a home			(Investments in longer-term instruments such as certificates of deposit, annuities, and retirement plans)									
21. Retirement												
22.												
23.												

Appendix D
Record of Monthly Expenses

		Jan	Feb	Mar	Apr	May	June
Church and charities							
Housing	rent or mortgage electric gas water telephone maintenance insurance taxes furnishings improvements other		(Use of a spiral notebook will enable you to record a full twelve months across two pages)				
Taxes							
Car	gas maintenance insurance licenses other		(Record each trip in a small notebook: date, mileage, purpose)				
Food (home and eating out)							
Clothing (purchase and care)							
Insurance (life and medical)							
Education							
Subscriptions							
Recreation and amusements							
Doctor and dentist							
Medicine and drugs							
Professional expenses	entertainment books and/or periodicals conferences continuing education office supplies professional clothing gifts other		(Keep receipts for entertainment items over $25, and record date, purpose, and persons present)				
Other							

Appendix E

Inventory of Family Resources

1. What are your family's goals?

2. How is your family using time, energy, and money to achieve these goals?

3. Enter the letters TM (Too Much), TL (Too Little), or AR (About Right) as appropriate in the right-hand columns, to indicate the present priorities as you see them.

Resource Inputs

Resource Expenditure Areas		Time	Physical and Psychic Energy	Money
Vocation (school, job, home chores)	husband			
	wife			
	child			
	child			
Family Relationships (talking, playing, or working together)	wife—husband			
	mother—child			
	father—child			
	total family			
Community Involvement (church, PTA, scouts, union, volunteer work)	husband			
	wife			
	child			
	child			
Recreation and Leisure	husband			
	wife			
	child			
	child			
Family Financial Planning	husband			
	wife			
	child			
	child			

Each family member is asked to complete the inventory in private, then bring it to a family conference for planning jointly the use of all resources. Each member evaluates all persons in the family separately. The whole family then works out its common definition of "Too Much," "Too Little," and "About Right." This inventory is not intended to prescribe the use of family resources but to help individuals discover and assess that use for themselves, for others, and for the family as a whole.

Appendix F

Determining Fair Salary for Clergy

1. Point of Reference

Intermediate Budget for Family of Four (Fall 1980) according to Bureau of Labor Statistics	$23,134
Add cost-of-living adjustment to present date	————
New point of reference (the new mid-point)	————

2. Range (as of Fall 1980)

Minimum (−20%)   Mid-point   Maximum (+20%)

18,508   19,664   20,821   21,977   23,134   24,290   25,447   26,603   27,760

3. Personal Proficiency Factors.

The mid-point, marked by the arrow at the outset, is a fair reference point at which to begin consideration of salary for a minister of average skills and performance who holds a three-year seminary degree and has about a dozen years of pastoral experience. The arrow may be moved incrementally to the left or to the right, depending on the personal proficiency factors of the minister: quality of service, years of experience, years of education and formal degrees earned, and skills constantly upgraded through continuing education.

4. Job Complexity Factors.

Size of Congregation: Move the arrow incrementally to the right at least half a mark for every 100 members over the base figure of 300 (possibly a lesser amount in the case of a multiple staff).

Size of Staff: Move the arrow incrementally to the right at least half a mark (in the case of the senior pastor only) for each full-time staff member being directly supervised.

5. Family Factors.

Family need is sometimes difficult to assess, but the number of dependents and the age of the children should in any case be considered.

6. Professional Factors.

Again difficult to assess; the salary levels of other professionals in the community (such as school or hospital administrators) may prove illuminating and helpful.

7. Fair Salary.

After being moved back and forth a few times, the arrow will indicate a fair salary for the minister for the current year. Remember that this amount embraces both cash salary and housing allowance.

Appendix G

Clergy Remuneration Schedule

	Minimum	Mid-Point	Maximum
1. Compensation			
A. Salary			
Cash salary	_____	_____	_____
Housing allowance	_____	_____	_____
Total Salary	_____	_____	_____
B. Benefits			
Pension program	_____	_____	_____
Health insurance	_____	_____	_____
Disability insurance	_____	_____	_____
Life insurance	_____	_____	_____
Social Security allowance	_____	_____	_____
Total Benefits	_____	_____	_____
Total Compensation	_____	_____	_____
2. Expenses of Ministry			
Transportation	_____	_____	_____
Continuing education	_____	_____	_____
Hospitality	_____	_____	_____
Books and periodicals	_____	_____	_____
Other	_____	_____	_____
Total Expenses of Ministry	_____	_____	_____

Notes

Page

ix. *The American Press wire service so reported in the *Progress Bulletin* (Pomona, Calif.: Progress Bulletin Publishing Company, 10 June 1980), p. 1.

x. *A 1972 study of attitudes concerning housing of clergy families in the East Ohio Conference of the United Methodist Church, done while I was serving as Area Director of Pastoral Care and Counseling, was published in the *Christian Advocate,* 18 January 1973, under the title "Laymen Think Parsonages OK—Clergy Want to Rent or Buy," pp. 7–9.

1. *Alvin Toffler, *The Third Wave* (New York: Bantam Books, 1981).

1. †*Data Track 4,* "Households and Families," Social Research Publication, American Council of Life Insurance, Washington, D.C. (Summer 1978).

3. *Judith S. Wallerstein and Joan B. Kelley, *Surviving the Breakup* (New York: Basic Books, 1980).

3. †Robert Fuller, "Inflation: The Rising Cost of Living on a Small Planet," Worldwatch Paper 34 (1980). Worldwatch Institute, 1776 Massachusetts Avenue, Washington, D.C. 20036.

4. *Fred Allvine, *The New State of the Economy: The Challenging Prospect* (Englewood Cliffs, N.J.: Winthrop, 1977).

5. *Most studies fail to show a relationship between size of income and degree of happiness. See Carin Rubenstein, "Money and Self-Esteem, Relationships, and Satisfaction," *Psychology Today* (May 1981): 29–44.

8. *Philip Zimbardo, "The Age of Indifference," *Psychology Today* (August 1980): 71.

10. *From Milton Rokeach and Seymour Parker, "Values as Social Indicators of Poverty and Race in America," *The Annals of the American Academy of Political and Social Science,* Vol. 388 (March 1970): 97–111.

11. *For additional values-clarification resources see the annotated bibliography; see also *Christians Doing Financial Planning,* a handbook prepared by the Commission on Stewardship of the National Council of Churches (1976), which describes several values-clarification schemes, including the one used above.

14, *See John Wesley's sermon on "The Good Steward" (Luke 16: 1–19), *Wesley's Standard Sermons,* 4th ed. (London: The Epworth Press, 1956), 2:461–80.

21. *See David L. Williamson, "We are Concerned," *The Christian Ministry* (May 1979): 34–35.

25. *A listing of trained and certified pastoral counselors or marriage and family counselors is available from the American Association of Pastoral Counselors, 3000 Connecticut Avenue, N.W., Suite 300, Washington, D.C. 20008, and the American Association for Marriage and Family Therapy, 924 West Ninth, Upland, California 91786.

34. *Reported in *The Progress Bulletin* (Pomona, Calif.: 10 June 1980), p. 1. The study was prepared by Research Forecast, Inc. for Americana Healthcare Corporation, which operates nursing homes in eleven states.

37. *Fabian Linden, "Magic Numbers—Ages 25 to 44 and Other Ages of Spending," *Consumers Magazine* (March 1978): 65–68.

39. *See also *Christians Doing Financial Planning.*

42. *See *Money in Our Children's Hands,* an educational packet produced by the American Council of Life Insurance, 1850 K Street, Washington, D.C. 20006.

47. *This formula for arriving at fair compensation for clergy was suggested by a friend and tax consultant, the Rev. Bobby Edwards, P.O. Box 1387, Ft. Collins, Colorado 80522.

48. *See the *Clergy Tax Guide* published annually by Abingdon Press, Nashville, Tennessee.

52. *See Fred Smoot, "Self-Perceived Effects of the Parsonage System on United Methodist Clergy and Spouses: Sense of Becoming and Growth," a School of Theology at Claremont, California, Ph.D. dissertation, (1978).

53. *Manfred Holck, Jr., "If You Want to Buy the Parsonage," *Church Management: The Clergy Journal* (January 1978). Reprints available from P.O. Box 1625, Austin, Texas 78767.

70. *For details about specific workshop designs write to the Program Director, Interfaith Council for Family Financial Planning, 1850 K Street, N.W., Washington, D.C. 20006.

Annotated Bibliography

Media

"The Clergy Family and Financial Planning" is a videotape produced by the Interfaith Media Center, Claremont, California. Six 30-minute presentations deal with the major concepts in financial planning, including the life cycle, remuneration and taxes, theological perspectives on money, protecting resources, financial institutions and credit, and psychology of money in the family. Available in ¾ inch Umatic, ½ inch VHS, or ½ inch Betamax formats. Write to the Interfaith Council for Family Financial Planning, 1850 K Street, N.W., Washington, D.C. 20006, for information regarding availability.

Simulation Game

"The Clergy Family Through the Life Cycle" is a simulation game created by Lance Barker and Richard Scheef. Write to the Interfaith Council for Family Financial Planning, 1850 K Street, N.W., Washington, D.C. 20006, for information on the use of the game.

Books

Armbruster, Dorothy M. *Pennies and Millions: A Woman's Guide to Saving and Investing Money.* Garden City, N.Y.: Doubleday, Inc., 1962. Written primarily for women to help them in the financial arena.

Barker, John C. *Personal Finances for Ministers.* Philadelphia: Westminster Press, 1973. Deals with salary contracts, negotiations, record keeping, spending plans, credit, investing, and retirement.

Bergler, Edmund. *Money and Emotional Conflicts.* New York: International University Press, 1959. Nontechnical; exposes some of the emotional conflicts caused by money.

Crook, Roger H. *Serving God with Mammon: The Economic Ministry of the Family.* Richmond, Va.: Covenant Life Curriculum Press, 1965. How we make and use our money in a values context.

Feldman, Frances L. *The Family in Today's Money World,* second edition. New York: Family Service Association of America, 1976. Excellent survey of the current economic milieu, the family life cycle, money and counseling, needs-assessment for families, and family resources.

Holck, Manfred, Jr. *Making It on a Pastor's Pay.* Nashville: Abingdon Press, 1979. Geared to helping pastors in the whole area of finances.

Knight, James. *For the Love of Money*. New York: Washington Square
  Press, 1978. Covers the more pathological dimensions of the use of
  money, from a Freudian perspective.
Margolius, Sidney. *Your Personal Guide to Successful Retirement*. New
  York: Random House, Inc., 1979. Six steps to successful retirement,
  with special attention to such matters as Social Security, pensions, and
  annuities.
Porter, Sylvia. *The Money Book*. New York: Avon Books, 1975. A com-
  prehensive guide to every phase of money management.
Raths, L., Harmon, M., and Simon, S. *Values and Teaching*. Columbus,
  Ohio: Charles E. Merrill, 1966. A basic introduction to values clarification; includes a variety of exercises and teaching strategies.
Simon, Sidney B. *Meeting Yourself Halfway*. Niles, Ill.: Argus Communications, 1974. Thirty-one values-clarification strategies.
Thal, Helen, and Holcombe, Melinda. *Your Family and Its Money,* revised
  edition. Boston: Houghton Mifflin, 1973. Especially addressed to teenagers for use in high-school curricula, deals with values as well as
  practical skills.

Booklets

Money and Credit Management Education, National Consumer Finance
  Association, 1000 Sixteenth Street, N.W., Washington, D.C. 20036,
  offers a variety of pamphlets and small books in all areas of finance.
Money Management Institute, Household Finance Corporation, Prudential
  Plaza, Chicago, Illinois 60601, produces many free booklets covering
  a range of finance issues, including credit and consumer guidelines,
  children's spending, housing, and autos.
Bibliography for Consumers. Everybody's Money, Box 431, Madison, Wis-
  consin 53701. A 48-page booklet listing books and pamphlets on bank-
  ruptcy, consumer protection, cooperatives, credit, food, frauds, health,
  money management, pensions, and wills.
*Christians Doing Financial Planning: A Handbook for Individuals and
  Families*. Commission on Stewardship, National Council of Churches,
  Presbyterian Center, 341 Ponce de Leon Avenue, N.E., Atlanta, Georgia
  30308, 1976. An excellent little workbook containing sample work
  sheets; highly recommended for use in workshops.
A Date with Your Future—Money Management for the Young Adult.
  Education and Community Services, American Council of Life Insurance,
  1850 K Street, N.W., Washington, D.C. 20006. One of many free publications offered by the American Council of Life Insurance. Write for
  a catalog of free and inexpensive publications in various areas of family
  financial planning.

Magazines

Changing Times. Kiplinger Family Services, Washington Editors, 1729 H
  Street, N.W., Washington, D.C. 20006. A monthly periodical covering
  current financial trends.
Consumer Reports. Consumer Union of the U.S., 256 Washington Street,
  Mt. Vernon, New York 10550. A monthly magazine dealing with con-
  sumer issues and providing product evaluations.